Going
Your Child Can Thrive in Public School

God brought David and Kelli Pritchard into my life at a time when the odds were against me. David and Kelli opened their home and their hearts to me, allowing me to watch and learn how a godly family lives and loves. I continually thank God for showing me all I could hope for, desire and have in a family.

Michael DeGraw
Teenager who lived with the Pritchards for a time

Going Public reveals the Pritchards' hearts for unconditional love and aggressive positive involvement by parents in their children's educational life, and provides many excellent suggestions for parents to use with regard to their interaction with schools. The Pritchards' insightful book is clearly founded on Christian principles and establishes the sort of connections all Christians should have with others—even those who serve at "government" schools. Parents who read *Going Public* may end up being better informed on schooling issues than the educational staff with whom they interact throughout their children's public-school experience. I heartily recommend this book to professional educators and parents alike.

Daniel C. Elliott, Ed.D.
Professor and Curriculum Specialist
Office of Distance Learning
Azusa Pacific University

Going Public is the right book at the right time for frazzled and frantic parents. I have known the Pritchard family as pastor and friend for more than 20 years. Their insights and experiences will bring purpose and peace to many lives.

Darcy Fast
Former Major League Baseball player
Senior Pastor, Centralia Community Church

The composure and poise that Tavita Pritchard showed when he was thrust into the national spotlight is the type of character quality that takes a lifetime of parenting to produce. I highly recommend this book and the message that the Pritchards have on parenting.

Jim Harbaugh
Stanford University Head Football Coach and Former NFL player

Over the past two decades, we have witnessed David and Kelli's wise, biblical and practical approach to raising their own children and countless others. You are holding an excellent tool for all parents who want to raise kids who will find and fulfill their God-given destiny.

Sam and Kathi Katina
The Katinas

As David and Kelli's pastor, I have had many opportunities to observe their lives up close. They are an amazing couple with a unique blend of passion and compassion for Jesus, life and people. I know that God will use the principles they have built their lives and family on as they share them with others.

Dr. Jim Kennington
Pastor, Lake City Community Church

While many Christian families fear the negative influence of public schools, the Pritchards remind us that we don't have to "take God into the public schools," because He's already there! Finally, a positive, practical book that encourages people to work together as a family and impact our schools and communities for Jesus.

Kjel and Leslie Kiilsgaard
Public high school teacher and coach
High school counselor

Christian parents sometimes agonize about issues related to their children's education—and often with good reason. *Going Public* is a wonderful resource that takes families beyond pat answers and "conventional wisdom." I especially encourage parents to instill in their kids the "Big Five," as the Pritchards recommend (see chapter 11). David and Kelli Pritchard provide practical content that will assist parents throughout their children's school years.

Alex McFarland, M.A., D.D.
President, Southern Evangelical Seminary and the Veritas Graduate School

If you want to find out what marriage and parenting is all about, just watch David and Kelli as they interact with each other and with their children. One of the things that strike me the most is the love and respect their children have for them. If the proof is in the pudding, you only have to watch the Pritchard family to see a model of a family that loves each other and the God who created them.

Bill Paige
Vice President and Special Assistant to the President of Young Life

As a coach, I am always looking for examples of devotion and self-control so that I can relate those qualities to our team. The Pritchard family is a perfect example of those qualities. I personally know all eight of the Pritchard children and have taught and coached two of them. They reach for the highest stars, knowing that if they fail, they will still hit the moon.

Jonathan B. Randall
Physical Education Instructor and Head Football and Baseball Coach
Clover Park High School

Because the Pritchards believe every child is of great value and worth, their home has become a refuge for many who have been forgotten. They have been able to give to "the forgotten" who have crossed their path and call them "friend."

Steven R. Ridgway
Executive Director, Northwest Network Foundation

David and Kelly Pritchard have been modeling good parenting for the last 20 years. Their methods are based on sound principles that will work in any culture and with any type of children. You will be blessed as you read their parenting strategies based on the concept that children are most fulfilled when their parents are in control.

Don and Robin Stuber
National Directors of Small Town Ministries, Young Life

Going Public is a must-read for anyone considering public education for their children. David and Kelli Pritchard remind us that the responsibility of raising our children begins and ends with their most influential teachers—parents.

Lynne Thompson
Author, *Official Soccer Mom Devotional*

What's a Christian parent to do when it comes to school choice? Should Christian parents homeschool, send their children to Christian school or enroll them in public school? I do not believe that there is one correct answer for all. However, for parents choosing public schools for formal education, *Going Public: How Your Child Can Thrive in Public School* is a must-read.

Parents need to saturate their homes with the truth of their faith 24/7 and play a major role in the daily formal education, whether that training takes place exclusively at home, in a Christian school, or in a public school. In Proverbs 22:6, parents are told to "train a child in the way he should go, and even when he is old he will not turn away from it." Training does not merely come from isolated formal training, but is the sum total of the life experiences.

The Pritchards point out the importance of teaching children the fear of the Lord, the need to obey parents, and the importance of maintaining self-control to thrive in the public-school environment. Further, they give practical tips on what to do and what to avoid. In the process, they tackle the tough issues, such as how to deal with sex education, the homosexual agenda, the roles of moms and dads, and the public-school campus as a mission field for believers.

Using biblical truths and practical examples, David and Kelli Pritchard have succeeded in writing a "how to" book about thriving in public schools.

Finn Laursen
Executive Director, Christian Educators Association International
www.ceai.org

goingpublic

YOUR CHILD CAN THRIVE
IN PUBLIC SCHOOL

David & Kelli Pritchard
with Dean Merrill

BakerBooks

a division of Baker Publishing Group
Grand Rapids, Michigan

Published by Baker Books
a division of Baker Publishing Group
P.O. Box 6287, Grand Rapids, MI 49516-6287
www.bakerbooks.com

Baker Books edition published 2014
ISBN 978-0-8010-1819-0

Previously published by Regal Books

Printed in the United States of America

Library of Congress Control Number: 2014954056

*This book is dedicated to all of the families
who deeply care about educating their children,
as well as the teachers and staff
who daily serve those students.*

Contents

Foreword

By Denny Rydberg, President of Young Life

Some called it the biggest upset in college football history. On October 6, 2007, underdog Stanford University beat top dog USC, 24-23, in front of a televised audience and 85,000 people in the Los Angeles Coliseum. In storybook fashion, the Stanford quarterback completed a touchdown pass in the end zone to tie the game with less than 50 seconds on the clock. And the kick was good! After the game, Stanford's new coach waved off reporters, saying, "Talk to Tavita. This is his day." Tavita Pritchard was the sophomore quarterback who had just made history with his first college start.

In an instant, Tavita was the bright eyes at the center of a sports media storm. Without hesitation, the 6'4", 200-pound Samoan smiled and said, "This is for my dad. He couldn't be here today because he had to perform a wedding. And all the glory goes to God."

Tavita's dad is the man who helped write this book. David and Kelli Pritchard raised the young man who made college history that day and impressed the sports world with his composure, his spirit and his smile. And Tavita is a product of public education.

Public-school parents, take heart! Not only is it possible for your kids to survive the public-school system in these United States, it's also possible for them to thrive and become fine men and women who make a positive impact on others. And in the process, it's possible for families of faith to help shape the public-school system and infuse it with the winsome fragrance of Jesus Christ.

I'm thrilled that you've opened this book. I've never seen another like it. This book was created to encourage moms and dads who—by design or by default—have chosen to send their kids to public schools. That includes Marilyn and me. We sent all four of our kids to public schools. It's not a book about bashing private schools or home schools or the people who support them. It's not a book about bashing anyone. It's a book about faith, hope and love and how the light of Jesus Christ can dispel shadows and warm hearts anywhere, even in a public school.

David and Kelli tell real-life stories from 24 years of raising eight children to love and follow Jesus Christ. With a warm and winsome spirit, they share principles that have guided the Pritchard parade through the twists and turns of public education with courage, creativity and joy. Not only have they survived the journey, they have also thrived along the way and left the life-giving imprint of Jesus on teachers, classmates and friends.

No one expected Stanford to beat USC on October 6, 2007. Stanford was projected to lose by 41 points. The starting quarterback was injured, and his replacement had only thrown three passes his entire college career. But then Tavita Pritchard surprised the world and helped make history with his team.

These days, not many people expect their kids to thrive in public schools. Many simply hope they will survive. But get ready for an upset. If you read this book and put the principles in practice, you might surprise the world and help make history with *your* team. In the meantime, you have a great cloud of witnesses cheering for you, and David and Kelli Pritchard are on the front row.

Acknowledgments

The most important thing to teach your child is also the most important Person for us to thank: the Lord our God.

We are grateful for the heritage our parents gave us—for the value they placed on educating their children.

Thank you to our friend Dean Merrill. Without his help, we wouldn't have been able to see this project completed.

To the incredible Miller and Pritchard clans, thank you for your unconditional love and support. We love and appreciate you all!

To our Young Life family—thank you for your friendship and encouragement.

To those friends (you know who you are) who have been parenting alongside us in the trenches, thank you for the lessons you have taught us and for partnering with us on this journey.

To all the children we claim as "ours," thank you for persevering as we have all grown together.

And certainly we want to acknowledge Alyse, Krista, Tavita, Jordan, Tana, Dani, Keila and Sina, for without you this journey might never have begun. We thank God every day for who we have become because of your presence in our lives.

CHAPTER 1

You Can Do It!

We were a little surprised that afternoon back in 1992 when the school principal's office called our home for the second time. We'd already been summoned earlier in the day to pick up Alyse, our third-grader, who had developed a fever. Now it was past three o'clock, and the message this time was about our first-grader.

"Mrs. Pritchard, Krista's here in the office, crying. She says that she's afraid to ride her bike home. Maybe you had better come down."

"That's not like her," I answered, alarmed. "She's usually pretty confident. Do you know what's the matter?"

"She says a group of third-grade boys have been harassing her and Alyse—we didn't know this was going on. She says they've yelled at the girls on their way home, called them names, shoved them and even spit on them. What really concerns me is that she says the boys showed them a knife one time."

"Well, that's certainly interesting! Let me call David, and one of us will be right over," I said, hanging up the phone.

The route to and from school was only a mile or so through quiet neighborhood streets in our pleasant town of Centralia, Washington. We had always assumed our kids were safe—but apparently not. I quickly dialed my husband at the pizza shop we operated at the time. I filled him in on what the principal had told me. "Do you think you could run and get Krista at school?" I pleaded. "I need to stay here with the two little ones."

"Wow! Okay, I'm on my way," he responded. "I'll find out more, and we'll talk about it when I get home."

When David came through the office door at school, our daughter jumped up to give him a big hug, still crying. "What's wrong, honey?" he said, picking her up. "Tell me why you're so upset." The two of them sat down together in a chair across from the principal.

"Tommy's going to hurt me!" she cried. "He'll push me off my bike if I ride home." Apparently our two girls had soldiered through the harassment when they were together. But on this day, Krista didn't dare try to ride the gauntlet alone. She was petrified.

"I'm very sorry, Mr. Pritchard," the principal declared, sincere concern in his voice. "I'm appalled . . . I had no idea this was occurring. We will certainly deal with the boys right away. I really think you should call the police and press charges."

David didn't commit himself. "Well, Kelli and I will talk to the girls and let you know later."

So *this* was what was happening these days to kids in public school! Here we thought we were fine in a town of only 12,000 people, more than an hour away from the Seattle-Tacoma metropolis. But now it seemed our children were at risk, even in the primary grades. How would they ever survive junior high and high school?

We knew that many of our friends at church and elsewhere had chosen to send their kids to private schools for just this very reason. Others were busy homeschooling their children. Would we need to follow their lead?

After David loaded up Krista's bike and brought her home, I gave her a comforting snack. He then returned to the pizza shop, where the evening rush would be starting soon. We didn't get to talk in depth until late that night. Finally, with all four kids in their beds and the house quieting down, we sank into the living room couch to reflect.

Right away, David said, "I just can't see us calling the police. What are they going to do—come out and arrest a couple of nine-year-olds?"

"I know," I said. "But we can't let this kind of thing go. You saw how scared Krista was today."

"Oh, definitely," he responded. "We have to do *something* about it. The question is, what?"

We kept talking. Eventually we came to the conclusion that, instead of expecting third parties—the principal or the police—to solve this problem, we should work it out ourselves. By the next day, we had learned that Tommy lived in a single-parent home. We also found a connection to him—we knew his uncle, who filled us in on some of the history.

We got Tommy's phone number, and my husband called his mom. When she answered, he said, "Hello, this is David Pritchard calling. I believe your son Tommy and my daughter Alyse are in the same class at school."

"Yes . . . ?" she answered guardedly.

He explained what had happened and what the principal had suggested. Then before she could reply, he continued, "What we would like to do is have Tommy and his Uncle Kevin come over to our house for lunch on Sunday. We've got four kids ourselves, so what's a couple more, you know? It would be good to get to know your son a little more, if that's okay with you."

"I suppose that would be all right," she said quietly.

"Great! Have them come at 12:30."

Little Krista was definitely nervous about all this, but we assured her that things would turn out okay. That day after church, we had a lively time over teriyaki chicken and rice, and of course Tommy was on his best behavior. No doubt he wondered if he was being softened up for a lecture once the meal was finished. Instead, David took Tommy outside to throw around a football—he had shared with us that he loved the game.

"Really?" David queried. "I love football, too! In fact, did you know I played for Washington State during college? We even went to the Holiday Bowl in 1981. It was a really high-scoring game against BYU. It looked for quite a while like we could take them, but in the end, we lost by just two points, 38 to 36." Tommy's eyes grew wide.

Later that day, as Tommy tried to hang on to David's tight spiral passes, he became more animated. David told him that football wasn't just a guy thing at the Pritchard house; the girls knew what to do with a pigskin, too. By the end of the visit, the boy had gained a whole new understanding of his classmate and her younger sister.

Thereafter, whenever we saw Tommy in the neighborhood or at school, we waved enthusiastically and asked how he was doing. He came to view us as his friends. Alyse and Krista told us in the following weeks that Tommy acted like he'd been appointed their personal protector.

God Is Bigger Than the Public School

Fifteen years have passed since that incident, and our family has doubled in size, to eight children. We've also moved to the big city. Today, Alyse is a 2006 graduate of the University of Southern California, majoring in English literature. She intends to apply to medical school. Krista more recently graduated from the University of Hawaii, earning an interdisciplinary degree in kinesiology and psychology. She also stretched her schedule to include classes in Samoan so that she could absorb more of her father's South Pacific heritage. Both girls, as well as their six siblings, were educated in the public-school system every step of the way—and they thrived.

We have faced challenges and complications, a lot of them far more serious than third-grade bullies. Our kids have endured teachers who have ridiculed anyone naïve enough to believe the Bible, coaches who have rewarded poor behavior and bad attitudes, and hostile classmates who have lashed out because our girls have taken a stand on social issues. We've talked together along the way, brainstormed together, researched together and prayed together. We've also rejoiced together as problems have been solved, relationships have been repaired and character has been formed. We have learned and relearned the lessons of that day long ago back in Centralia:

- God has a reason for allowing each "Tommy" into our family's life. Our approach to these difficult people and situations is, *We can learn something here.*

- The most important individuals we need to teach and guide are not other people's kids, but our own.

- To each antagonist, family and school, we can demonstrate the love of Christ. The hurting world needs this witness more than anything else.

- Whatever tough situations come along, we will get through them together as a family. No one is in this struggle alone.

- God is always in charge. As Jesus said to His "family" of disciples just a few hours before a crisis struck, "In this world you will have trouble. But take heart! I have overcome the world" (John 16:33).

We are more convinced than ever before, after 18 years of public-school experiences with our children (and at least a dozen yet to go!), that God is bigger than the modern educational monolith. He is on the side of the children He created, and He is not nervous. He is sovereign, after all.

If Christian parents in the old Soviet Union, or in the anti-Christian nations of today, have managed to raise godly children despite the pressures of a hostile school system, we on this continent have little excuse. "The one who is in you is greater than the one who is in the world," wrote the apostle John, while living in a pagan, idol-worshiping Roman Empire (1 John 4:4). This promise is still true in the twenty-first century.

How does God protect and nurture boys and girls in the public-school environment? What is His strategy for overcoming the difficulties they face? The main answer is this: *parents*. We who brought them into this world hold the keys to getting them safely through childhood and adolescence. God equips us—just ordinary dads and moms—to equip and fortify our kids. In so doing, we set them up to face adulthood with strength and conviction. Starting in the very first classroom, our home, we teach them to be the influencers rather than the influenced.

Quiz Time

It's interesting—almost humorous—the kinds of questions people ask when they learn we have eight children. We've heard all kinds of odd comments over the years, accompanied by quizzical looks. But even more humorous than the comments are the questions.

"Are you Catholic?" No.

"Are you Mormon?" No.

"Oh, is this a case of *his, hers* and *ours*?" No, we're not a blended collection from previous marriages.

Other questions get a little more personal: "Don't you know what causes them?" Yes, we're fully educated on the process of conception!

"How are you ever going to pay for all that college?" Ask us this one later; we're still in the thick of it.

Recently, a newer stereotype has manifested itself: "Are you into that homeschooling thing?" You can see the questioner imagining us growing a huge garden, grinding our own grain and sewing all our own clothes.

We smile at the question. Then we reply enthusiastically, "Yes! We *definitely* homeschool our children . . . and starting at age five, we also send them to public school to get more information."

We consider ourselves to be our children's number-one educators, and we will never give up that responsibility or privilege—even though they spend 30 hours a week in somebody else's classroom. We instruct our kids every day. We look for the teachable moments that intersect with what they are experiencing outside our home. We draw frames around their encounters and activities, showing how they fit within God's greater perspective.

The truth is, Kelli has a college degree in secondary education from Indiana State University and would have made an excellent homeschool teacher. Sometimes we've looked with a touch of jealousy at the flexible schedule that homeschoolers enjoy. But we have never felt released to pull away from the public school. We have seen so many benefits in that environment, so many chances for our children to grow, that we've determined to stay put. As we've talked with them about what has been at stake and what would please God most in test after test, their decision-making abilities have flowered right before our eyes.

And remember, we don't exactly live in the Bible Belt. We're more than 2,000 miles in the opposite direction, in a state that usually comes in dead last in U.S. church attendance statistics. (Sometimes our neighbor to the south, Oregon, kicks us up to forty-ninth place.) But we haven't let that dissuade us. We have believed, and are proving, that believing parents can raise kids with strong spiritual roots in the midst of a secular culture.

In one seminar we attended, a professional counselor stood up and boldly stated, "Never, never, never trust a teenager! I don't care what they tell you or how great they look, don't be fooled. Kids this age are not to be trusted." We were so offended! What an odd way to build any kind of relationship with your high schooler.

We looked at each other and shook our heads, because our view is exactly the opposite. We know what we've built into our kids over the years. That is why we can trust our kids at the Friday night football game, at the mall or on a date—unless they give us a clear reason not to do so. They know that we expect obedience and right choices. They know what our family believes and why we believe it.

Too many parents today operate under a premise of "I need to keep controlling the environment because I don't entirely trust my kid *in* the environment." This attitude affects everything from school choices to moral decisions. Most parents may not be as accusatory as the seminar speaker, but the underlying fear is the same. They worry constantly about how their son or daughter is going to behave if the fences are ever lifted.

The problem is this: What happens at age 18? Will that child suddenly become mature and trustworthy overnight?

Hardly.

We've always said we would much rather have Alyse, Krista, Tavita, Jordan, Tana, Danielle, Keila and Sina mess up at age 5 or 10 or 15, when the stakes are smaller, so that we can deal with the fallout right away. Our prayer, in fact, is borrowed from a wise mother: "Lord, we pray for us all, catch us early in our sin." The sooner mistakes and deliberate wrongdoing come to light, the sooner we can confess, repent and rise above our weakness.

Parents who are not paying attention, on the other hand, are in for rude awakenings as kids get older. In our work with Young Life, a nondenominational ministry to teenagers, we see the ugly fruit of what sociologists call "systemic abandonment." Most adults in our society used to accept their role in preparing children for adulthood. Over the past 50 years, things have changed dramatically. Many of today's adults are so busy making a living, chasing good times and dealing with their own relational messes that they give little attention to kids. Young people are abandoned, left to fend for themselves, trying to figure out how life actually works.

Not long ago we heard a teenager exclaim with disgust, "My parents don't care what I do!" Today, three different teenaged girls in our community come by our house all the time. Their fathers are in prison, and each of them has shared the pain and frustration of life with a mom who is so busy working and taking care of herself that there's no time left to be a parent.

Don't think this happens just in "certain families." Systemic abandonment cuts across all income levels, ethnic groups and regions of the country.

God's heart is broken as this tragedy unfolds. He longs for adults to live up to their calling, a large part of which is nurturing the next generation and preparing them to face the world with character and purpose. We strongly believe that the public school can be an early training ground—a place where our children have an opportunity to develop that character and find their purpose.

On the Hook

When the two of us jointly lead seminars for parents, we often do an exercise called Stand Where You Stand. We draw an imaginary line from one side of the room to the other and then ask participants to come stand along the line, indicating their view on a controversial statement, such as "Spanking is the best form of discipline." We tell the crowd, "Okay, this end of the continuum represents one extreme, while the opposite end represents the other. Now get out of your chairs and *stand where you stand.*" Once people have taken their positions at the left, center or right, we then pass around the microphone and have them explain their various views on the matter. It's always enlightening and gets everyone's mind in gear.

Here is another statement we've often used: "A teenaged boy ends up on the street, homeless and hooked on drugs. Whose fault is it—his parents' or his own?" For some in the crowd, this is an easy exercise. They march right away to the "teenager" end of the continuum. When we ask why, they say things like, "Hey, he's a big kid now; he makes his own choices in life. You can't blame the parents for what a 16-year-old decides to do with his money or his friends." Others, however, are not so sure about that. They stand puzzling and murmuring about where to stand on the imaginary line. We sometimes have to force them to commit themselves. They believe parents bear a great responsibility in shaping a child's life, but they hesitate to accept the guilt that goes along with that opinion.

Some will say, "No matter what you do, your child can still turn out bad"—which is quite true. But everyone in the room knows that this can be used as an alibi for negligent parenting.

If we're speaking to a Christian group, we may read the familiar proverb that says, "Train a child in the way he should go, and when he is old he will not turn from it" (Prov. 22:6). Now here's the question: Is this proverb a *promise* or a *generality*? In other words, does it carry the force of a contract with God—if you train your child correctly, he or she *will* follow in the right path? Or is it more of a general observation about how things normally work out in life? *Stand where you stand . . .*

Most of us agonize over this one. What's really going on inside is a wrestling match over how much responsibility we are willing to accept for raising our kids. We know that nobody can do a perfect job of parenting. But don't our efforts play a major role? Of course they do. Deep inside, we can't just chalk everything up to the child's free will or divine sovereignty. We know we're on the hook for at least some of the outcome.

Maybe it's best if we intellectually interpret this verse as a generality but live day to day as if it were a promise! How we parent our kids *does* matter. We make a difference in the way our children will go, in the paths they will take. We cannot escape the fact that we have at least *some* role to play, *some* influence to lend. No matter what our culture says, no matter how many psychological cartwheels we perform, God made a statement here that we cannot sidestep. He drew a direct connection between our actions and our children's character. If it were all a matter of chance, God would instead have told us simply to pray hard and cross our fingers. He did not. If it were solely a matter of genetic hard-wiring, He would have said, "Don't worry about it. The kid's gonna do what the kid's gonna do, and that's all there is."

Instead, God asked us to *do* something. That something is to train our children. God would not have asked us to attempt the impossible. He must have meant that we could succeed at this assignment.

The Biggest Leverage

Why spend so much space making this point? Because many modern parents, Christian and non-Christian alike, live with the assumption that what happens "out there" in the culture has more impact on their child than what happens "in here" in the family. They have bought into the myth that parents have little control over the factors that shape a child. That simply is not true.

God has placed us in a position to have more influence than all the outside factors combined. At the end of time, we will not be able to stand before God and beg off by saying that Hollywood or MTV or MySpace.com or the school board's secular humanists were just too strong for us to fight. *We* hold the levers of power. *We* have access to more hours per week with our child than any outsider. *We* must put that time to good use.

And when we do, God works with us to foster amazing strengths in our children. He helps us in guiding them to distinguish between "average" and "normal." These two words are not synonyms at all. Just because an attitude or behavior is common ("average") among today's youth population does not mean it should be accepted. The "average" teenager may rebel against his or her parents and other authority, but that doesn't make it right or even "normal." Kids can understand this, if we make it clear.

Public school, believe it or not, can actually be a great place for kids to observe and sort out these issues. As they engage the culture and interact with a diverse crowd of people, they come to see how the world functions, what leads to success and what is a dead-end street. Personally speaking, we would much rather have the Pritchard clan work through this process while they're under our care, hearing our perspective, seeing how the Word of God explains reality and morals and maturity, than to have them start the process when they're 18 years old and 500 miles away living in a university dorm. We want to be close to them during this critically important phase of their lives.

Dennis McCallum, a pastor at Xenos Christian Fellowship in Columbus, Ohio, drew an insightful analogy a few years ago:

> None of us who have children want them to drown. But how can we prevent it?

One way is to keep them away from bodies of water deeper than two feet. It works. Kids won't drown if they don't get into deep water.

But we can also guard them from drowning by another method: teaching them to swim. Though it isn't foolproof, it works rather well and provides more freedom.

In the same way, we should teach our kids to "swim" against the currents of the world. Avoidance of the world is ineffective—children eventually go away to college or start their own lives and encounter all the things we guarded them from.

They will be more ready to face worldly currents if we have taught them to swim.[1]

The rest of this book will provide, in a sense, swimming lessons. They are based on the premise that the public school is an excellent pool in which to train our young sons and daughters. Yes, it's deep and noisy and the water's cold and sometimes the chlorine gets in your eyes. Sometimes you get splashed by other swimmers. But this is preparation for even bigger bodies of water to come. Someday they'll have to swim in Lake Michigan or Puget Sound. Might as well get started learning now.

You can do it!

Note

1. Dennis McCallum, "The Postmodern Puzzle," *The Real Issue*, March 1998. http://www.leaderu.com/real/ri9802/mccallum.html (accessed October 2007).

CHAPTER 2

Is Public Education an Evil Plot?

One of the wonderful things about this country is the freedom to draw your own conclusions and say exactly what you think. For example . . .

According to Houston attorney Bruce N. Shortt:

> The government's schools have become foundries of ignorance and bad character. Surely few are wholly unaware that the government's schools are the nation's largest pusher of psychotropic drugs. . . . Violent crime and sexual abuse of students in the government's schools are far from uncommon. . . . [They] now incorporate curricula and programs that both are a threat to our children's physical and psychological health and are, in many instances, pornographic.[1]

His 2004 book is titled *The Harsh Truth About Public Schools*. He also hosts a blog and is frequently quoted in the media with such forthright statements as, "The little red schoolhouse has really become the little white sepulcher . . . a seething cauldron of spiritual, moral and academic mythologies."[2]

In both 2004 and 2005, Shortt and a Virginia cosponsor presented the nation's largest Protestant denomination, the Southern Baptist Convention, with a resolution that "encourage[d] all officers and members . . . to remove their children from the government schools" and seek "Christian alternatives."[3] The resolutions did not pass, but they drew widespread discussion and media attention.

Joel Turtel, author of *Public Schools, Public Menace*, shares Shortt's sense of alarm. He believes the public-school concept is not only horribly misguided, but even unpatriotic. "Local and state governments that claim the right to control our children's education," he writes, "also claim, in effect, that they own our children's minds and lives for twelve years. That is an appallingly arrogant claim, especially in America."[4]

It all sounds dire, even vicious. Has the entire public education enterprise become a vast conspiracy to undermine the mental and moral health of innocent children? Every conscientious and caring parent wants to know.

What Do the Facts Tell Us?

As Americans, we believe that everyone has the right to a fair trial, to due process, with the burden of proof on the accuser, not the accused. With this in mind, when it comes to the issue of the public-school system, let's take a step back from the rhetoric. Let's carefully examine the facts to see if public education is "guilty as charged"—or if there's another side of the story, one that might lead us to embrace a different verdict.

1. "Government Schools" Have Been Around a Long Time

The idea of a society *working together* to educate its young goes back for centuries. "The roots of America's system of public education extend as far back as ancient Greece and Rome and post-Renaissance Europe," writes Dr. Roselle K. Chartock in her book *Educational Foundations*. "Most of today's education practices and ideas have historic and global roots. . . . Often what appears to be new and exciting in education is not really a major change of any kind but actually a reappearance of an historically expanded concept."[5]

An early advocate of public education was seventeenth-century Moravian bishop John Amos Comenius, who said:

> Not the children of the rich or of the powerful only, but of all alike, boys and girls, both noble and ignoble, in all cities and towns, villages and hamlets, should be sent to school. . . . No one doubts that those who are stupid need instruction, that they may shake off their natural dullness. But in reality those who are clever need it far more, since an active mind, if not occupied with useful things, will busy itself with what is useless, curious, and pernicious.[6]

Comenius was noted throughout Europe for his educational passion—he was even famous in the New World, where he was asked to be the first president of Harvard (he declined).

The first American town to set up a taxpayer-funded public school was Dedham, Massachusetts, on the southwest side of Boston, in 1643 (a couple of nearby towns dispute this claim today, saying they were first by a few months). Children needed to learn to read, it was decided, in order to understand the Bible. The first Dedham teacher was a minister, the Rev. Ralph Wheelock, who received 20 pounds per year to instruct the youth of the community. Bear in mind that this was fewer than 25 years after the Pilgrims landed, long before George Washington and the other Founding Fathers were even born.

It was a seminal step for the colonists, one that would shape the kind of society they wanted to be. Looking back on this time in history, James Russell Lowell, the nineteenth-century poet and commentator, noted, "It was in making education not only common to all, but in some sense compulsory on all, that the destiny of the free republics of America was practically settled."[7]

After the Revolution, one of the early laws passed by the young U.S. Congress was the Land Ordinance of 1785, which detailed how real estate would be handled on the western frontier—and effectively established the public-school system. This ordinance declared that surveyors should mark off townships 6 miles wide and 6 miles long, subdivided into 36 sections of 1 square mile each. Congress went on to declare that Section 16, right in the middle of the township, should be set aside for maintaining a public school. In years to come across America, many a country schoolhouse was built on those mile-square plots of land.

The push for universal *free* education picked up momentum through the 1830s forward, led by Massachusetts's Horace Mann, among others. By 1870, every state provided free elementary schooling. The system's expansion "from one in which only well-to-do white males were educated into one that is tax-supported, with access for all" was by then complete.[8]

In today's world, we sometimes forget that some countries still have not made it this far. They struggle to find the funding and to create the political consensus needed to provide a basic education to every child. According to UNESCO, more than 100 million children in the world, including at least 60 million girls, have *no* access to primary schooling. Nearly a billion adults (one out of fewer than seven) are illiterate; two-thirds of these are women.[9]

Only in 1997 was Uganda able to guarantee a free seat in primary school (first through seventh grade) across the nation to a maximum of four children per family (on the premise that at least these students could go home in the evening and tutor any remaining brothers and sisters). This provision, mind you, put Uganda in the forefront of its African neighbors. Our Western assumption is that there's a free public school just down the road for everybody's kids, but this is just not yet a reality in some parts of the globe. Parents there can only look across the ocean at our system, and wish.

2. Test Scores Need a Context

Exhibit A in the criticism of public schools is the current state of standardized test scores. According to E. Roy Moore, Jr., author of the book *Let My People Go: Why Parents Must Remove Their Children from Public Schools Now*, "American schools are the best funded in the world. Yet out of 41 nations, American students consistently rank near or at the bottom in mathematics, physics and science."[10] Moore's rallying point is a movement he calls the Exodus Mandate.

Certainly American public schools need to do better. No one should be complacent or accept the mistaken notion that students are learning as well or as much as they could. However, the situation may not be as morbid as we are sometimes led to believe. Paul Farhi wrote recently in *The Washington Post*, "No nation included in the major international rankings educates as many poor students or as ethnically diverse a population as does the United States. Yet even as the percentage of historically low-achieving students has increased, our test scores have risen."[11] In America, we don't only test the cream of the crop. We test everybody in the room—and the room includes an ever increasing number of students for whom English is a second language, those whose parents forgot to provide breakfast that day, and those who suffer from other hindrances to the educational process. Their scores figure into the equation, too.

Farhi goes on to say, "When compared with students in the world's most industrialized nations, U.S. students were on par with the others . . . (and outperformed everyone in civics). Every Western country, not just the U.S., lagged behind Japan in math and science, suggesting that the 'achievement gap' in these subjects is an East-West phenomenon rather than an American one."[12]

At the end of the day, are we to be more concerned about placing twelfth instead of first—or should we be more interested in serving all kids, even those who have historically been marginalized? Test scores are important, but so is the inclusion of all parts and pieces that make up this wonderful place called America.

Our family happens to live in a school district with two high schools of nearly identical size, one of which racks up better test score numbers than the other. Does it surprise you that the superior performer has just 26 percent of its student body classified as "economically disadvantaged," while the lower performer has 51 percent?[13] We happen to personally know a number of faculty members in both schools, and they are quality instructors. They give their best every day. They simply have clientele with very different needs, problems and priorities coming in the front door.

Our family, though technically residing in the first high school's attendance zone, has deliberately sought and gotten a waiver to attend the second school—even though it means no bus service. Some people think we're crazy for doing this. But we happen to believe that the greater ethnic and economic diversity of the second school provides our kids with a rich educational experience. We *want* them to mix with all kinds of kids from all kinds of backgrounds. And as for the school's lower academic test scores—well, it didn't seem to hinder our first three kids from getting into USC, Hawaii and Stanford, respectively.

Amid all the negative press about American public-school test scores, the Council on Competitiveness, a Washington, DC-based business advisory group, reports that over the past two decades, the U.S. economy has grown faster than that of any other advanced nation, generating a third of the world's economic growth.[14] It was just about two decades ago (1983) that the members of the National Commission on Excellence in Education submitted their report, *A Nation at Risk: An Imperative for Educational Reform*, to the U.S. Secretary of Education. In its pages, they warned the American people that "a rising tide of [educational] mediocrity . . . threatens our very future as a nation."[15]

Well, those "mediocre" high-school graduates of the early '80s are now turning 40 and are presumably at the helm of our current economy, hailed by the Council on Competitiveness.

This does not mean that we should relax and assume all is well in the arena of public-school achievement. But the facts do tell us that many graduates of public schools are succeeding and helping to drive this nation forward. Perhaps it is fair to criticize our public education system, but isn't it also fair to appreciate what we have?

3. Today's Public Schools Do Have Some Ungodly Elements

We are the first to admit that the curriculum today is not as righteous as the texts Rev. Wheelock used to teach the children of Dedham back in 1643. Gone are the prayers that once marked the beginning of each school day, and the Ten Commandments once on the wall. As our national population has grown more culturally and religiously diverse, with immigrants from many lands and faith backgrounds, public educators have dialed back the openly Christian components of the school day. Some people are even fussing about the wording of the Pledge of Allegiance ("under God").

Some principals and teachers have overreacted by banning virtually all religious expression on school property. They have had to be informed by parents and attorneys that the individual student has a Constitutionally protected right to his or her own personal religious beliefs, and must not be prevented from talking, writing or singing about them. The Christian Educators Association International (www.ceai.org), among others, does a good job of clarifying what expressions of faith are still legally acceptable in America's government institutions.[16]

Other educators have assumed the role of missionary for their brand of godless politics and/or libertine ethics in the class-room, choosing textbooks and other supplemental materials accordingly. It is not uncommon for public-school teachers—and the school as a body—to promote the idea that homosexual be-havior is normal. And this is often just the tip of the iceberg. Throughout this book we will consider how to respond to the occasional teacher who thinks he or she "knows better" than parents or the community about what kids should learn when it comes to various moral issues.

The behavior of some teachers is troubling as well. The gamut runs from occasional foul language to high-profile cases of sexual intimacy with students. We live only a half-hour's drive from Des Moines, Washington, where in 1997 sixth-grade teacher Mary Kay Letourneau, a married mother of four, made national headlines for conceiving not one but two daughters with a student. Their affair began when he was just 13 years old. She received a 7-year prison sentence for statutory rape. Today she is no longer teaching (thank goodness); instead, she married the young man as soon as she got out of jail and he turned 21.[17]

This kind of sickening abuse disheartens us all. But before we generalize about public-school teachers, let us be honest enough to admit that private-school faculty members have their failures, too. Janelle Bird, a 20-something biology teacher at East Hill Christian School in Pensacola, Florida, went to prison for 2 years after being found guilty of having an affair with a 15-year-old student. She told the court she still loved the boy, and there was "nothing lewd or lascivious" about the situ-ation.[18] Fortunately, no professional code of conduct—public school or otherwise—condones this kind of behavior. A standard of propriety still exists, even if it is occasionally violated.

4. Public Schools Have a Ton of Good, Hardworking People

The "bad apples in the barrel" do not negate the presence of 2.7 million other hard-working, law-abiding, generally straight-living teachers in the public schools of this nation who mainly just want to help kids. They go to work day after day, semester after semester, because they love it. Or at least they did before society got into the habit of blaming them for much of what's wrong in the world today.

These teachers certainly don't do it for the money. Their salaries are scandalously low when compared to what we lavish on professional athletes, singers and comedians. What drives teachers is the reward of seeing a child "get it," of steering a teenager to make a good choice, of watching one of their alumni rise to prominence in the community.

Watch any popular movie about a brave teacher, from the now-classic *Stand and Deliver* (1988) to the more recent *Freedom Writers* (2007) and beyond. Such films remind us that public-school teachers are honorable people doing valuable work for the benefit of us all. They're not perfect, of course. But neither are they despicable.

For hundreds of thousands of teachers, their job is an expression of their Christian calling. They pray in their cars on the way to school in the morning, hoping that the love of Jesus will be evident in their words and actions. They take seriously what Christ said about not causing a single one of "these little ones" to stumble (see Matt. 18:6). Some volunteer after hours to lend a hand at meetings of Young Life, Youth for Christ or the Fellowship of Christian Athletes. They yearn for the support of Christian parents and fellow church members as they work in a demanding environment.

Tim Gilmore is a friend of ours who has been teaching at Centralia High School in Southwest Washington for more than 35 years. He was inspired long ago by Guy Dowd, National Teacher of the Year in 1986, who said that he started each day praying over the seating chart for his classroom, asking God to help him see and hear each child. Following Guy's lead, Tim has prayed for thousands of kids whose names have appeared on his seating charts. No, he hasn't been able to convince every student to make a decision for Christ, but he has been able to live his life before these impressionable kids in a way that has made a difference.

One of those kids was Jon Wiley, who as an adult says that he wouldn't be where he is today if it weren't for the influence of Mr. Gilmore. And where is he today? He's a successful pharmacist, happily married with six beautiful kids. At the time of this writing, Jon and his oldest daughter are getting ready to head to Cambodia on a mission trip.

Another student, Amanda Deal, who escaped a drug-addicted mom and fatherless home to live with her aunt and uncle in Centralia, wrote to Mr. Gilmore:

> I've never had anybody give me religious advice with their head on straight . . . you believe in something, and you believe so strongly. . . . and I always wondered how could you be wrong. Right now I'm seeking, and you've helped me a lot. . . . I think you're a great person and you should keep on doing what you're doing.

Jon and Amanda are not alone in their praise of Tim Gilmore. Check out what other former students have had to say:

- Cassie: "I gave my life to the Lord when I got to school on September 24, 2004. You are part of my testimony!"

- Treasa (regarding Father's Day): "Just a few years with you makes up for the loss of my real father."

- Elizabeth: "I love your faith in God and how you openly express it."

- A guy named Lavern: "[Without you] I don't think I would have the great outlook, dedication and passion for my relationships, work performance and attitude toward life."

- Kristen: "I know you are [having] an impact on kids, even though they seem untouched. Just keep the Lord shining through in your work! He works through you."

- Katie: "Even when I was being irrational, you were on my side. You . . . guided me away from . . . bad thoughts and taught me always to look on the bright side of any situation."

God is using the Tim Gilmores of the world to change kids forever. We simply cannot omit this from the public-school equation.

5. Like It or Not, 9 out of 10 Kids Today Go to a Public School

For the above reasons and many others, the plain statistics are that more than 47 million American children and youth are enrolled in public schools from kindergarten through grade 12.[19] That's about 89 percent of all American school kids. *And this ratio is not declining.* The previous numbers for the year 2000 were virtually the same.[20]

Even E. Ray Moore, author of *Let My People Go*, estimates (to his dismay) that more than 80 percent of *evangelical Christians* still place their children in public schools, despite a half-century of the Christian school movement and at least 25 years of the homeschooling phenomenon. Perhaps many of these parents have no Christian school in their town, or feel unable to afford the cost. Perhaps they would like to homeschool but don't feel qualified for the job. We venture to guess, however, that many of these parents simply do not agree that the public school is an evil establishment, and therefore unacceptable. They believe they can continue to work with the local school as they guide their children to a responsible adulthood that includes—is centered on—a love for God.

Though it can sometimes feel like "everybody's leaving the public schools," the numbers simply do not bear this out. Millions of families are still there—and intend to remain. It is primarily for these families that this book was written.

Focus on What's Within Reach

Rather than stressing over the big picture and disparaging the national trends, it is far more productive to focus on the things we individual parents can control, here at close range. What can we do to make good things happen in the education of our own one or two or three (or eight!) children? How can we prepare them to reap the benefits that the local public school has to offer? At the same time, how can we sensitize them to screen out the negatives? The apostle Paul wrote to one group of Christians, "Test everything. Hold on to the good. Avoid every kind of evil" (1 Thess. 5:21-22). How shall we practice that in our own families when it comes to our children's education?

As we seek to answer this question, let's stop and remind ourselves of an oft-forgotten fact: The public-school system in America is closely tied to the grassroots—probably more than any other government organization. In our community here in Lakewood, for example, decisions about the education of 11,000 students lie in the hands of a school board of five local members. We all know who they are; we see them at Starbucks and at the dry cleaners. We say hello and talk about anything on our minds. If we don't like something, we know their phone numbers. And that's important to us, because these five people are the ones who hire and fire the school superintendent, set policy and shape the district's budget. Obviously they are bound by certain federal and state laws, but within those guidelines they have tremendous power to determine what happens in our children's classrooms. Where else in government does this much power reside at the local level?

If we want a change of board stance or perspective, all it takes is one well-run election campaign. Within a few weeks, a new member can be elected, changing 20 percent of the whole. It's not that hard. We don't have to go through six layers of bureaucracy. We don't have to drive to Olympia (our state capital) or fly to Washington, DC. We can affect the future of public education right here in our own backyard.

Beyond the board level, the opportunities for parental influence are everywhere. We are not helpless. When a levy or bond issue comes up, we can make our voice heard. Any time a large group of parents shows up at a school board meeting, the impact is immediate. All it takes is getting off our comfortable couches and taking initiative.

Harvard professor Robert D. Putnam wrote a national bestseller a few years ago titled *Bowling Alone: The Collapse and Revival of American Community.* He notes how less connected we seem to be with one another these days, as evidenced by far fewer bowling leagues (compared to the 1960s), though *individual* bowling continues at a steady pace. Putnam's book is chock full of statistics and charts that demonstrate his point.

He developed what he termed the "Social Capital Index," a measure of how much residents trust other people, join organizations (from Rotary Club to the church choir), volunteer, vote and socialize with friends. Then he analyzed what difference this makes in politics, the workplace, religion, philanthropy, crime—and education. The results were startling:

Those states with high social capital have measurably better educational outcomes than do less civic states. The Social Capital Index is highly correlated with student scores on standardized tests taken in elementary school, junior high, and high school, as well as with the rate at which students stay in school. The beneficial effects of social capital persist even after accounting for a host of other factors that might affect state educational success. . . . Astonishingly, social capital was the single most important explanatory factor.[21]

In other words, in communities where adults care and connect with each other, talking to each other about how things are going and what might be improved, report cards brighten up. But when adults in any given community stay aloof, refusing to interact with each other and the local institutions, hunkering down in their homes to complain about all of "them" down at the school, the police station, city hall, the board of education and so on, kids tend to do more poorly in the classroom. (Putnam's graph of the 50 states, showing low-to-high performance in light of the Social Capital Index, is absolutely fascinating—North Dakota gets the best marks, in case you're wondering!)

The public-school establishment, though large and complicated and sometimes frustrating, is not a closed fortress. It can be influenced. When we parents and other taxpayers see the need for improvement, we can take action; our hands are not tied. The levers of power are within our reach. We can bring our values to the public-school arena—to the boardroom, to the principal's office, to the parent-teacher association, to the individual classroom desk. We can make things better.

In thinking about the public schools, we would do well to heed the ancient wisdom given to the prophet Isaiah some 2,800 years ago:

Do not call conspiracy everything this people calls conspiracy; do not fear what they fear, and do not dread it. The LORD Almighty is the one you are to regard as holy, he is the one you are to fear, he is the one you are to dread . . . I will wait for the LORD . . . I will put my trust in him (8:12-13,17).

Which brings us to the central point of the next chapter.

Notes

1. Bruce Shortt, "Will Your Kids Be Christian?" World Net Daily, December 20, 2005. http://www.worldnetdaily.com/news/article.asp?ARTICLE_ID=48001 (accessed October 2007).

2. Bruce Shortt, quoted in J. Grant Swank, Jr., "Homeschool? Public School? Where's God?" MichNews.com, January 31, 2005. http://www.michnews.com/cgi-bin/artman/exec/view.cgi/100/6678 (accessed October 2007).

3. "Baptists: Plan Exit from Government Schools," World Net Daily, April 26, 2006. http://www.worldnetdaily.com/news/article.asp?ARTICLE_ID=49910 (accessed October 2007).

4. Joel Turtel, *Public Schools, Public Menace: How Public Schools Lie to Parents and Betray Our Children* (Staten Island, NY: Liberty, 2005), p. 164.

5. Roselle K. Chartock, *Educational Foundations: An Anthology* (Upper Saddle River, NJ: Pearson Prentice Hall, 2nd ed., 2003), p. 64.

6. John Amos Comenius, *Didactica magna,* published in Latin in 1628, available in English as M. W. Keatinge, *The Great Didactic of John Amos Comenius* (Kila, MT: Kessinger Publishing, 2005).

7. James Russell Lowell, "New England Two Centuries Ago," *Literary Essays,* vol. 2 (1870-1890).

8. Chartock, *Educational Foundations: An Anthology,* p. 65.

9. UNESCO, "World Declaration on Education for All," affirmed March 9, 1990, in Jomtien, Thailand. http://www.unesco.org/education/efa/ed_for_all/background/jomtien_declaration.shtml (accessed October 2007).

10. E. Ray Moore, Jr., *Let My People Go: Why Parents Must Remove Their Children from Public Schools Now* (Greenville, SC: Ambassador-Emerald International, 2002), back cover.

11. Paul Farhi, "Five Myths About U.S. Kids Outclassed by the Rest of the World," *The Washington Post,* January 21, 2007, B-02. http://www.washingtonpost.com/wp-dyn/content/article/2007/01/19/AR2007011901360_pf.html (accessed October 2007).

12. Ibid.

13. "Washington Public Schools and Districts: Tacoma," at School Data Direct. http://www.schoolmatters.com/app/search/q/stype=SM/stid=48/llid=116/locname=/ ctyname=Tacoma/zip=/dst=/adv=false/page=/site=pes (accessed October 2007).

14. The Council on Competitiveness, *U.S. Competitiveness 2001: Strengths, Vulnerabilities and Long-term Priorities*. http://www.compete.org/pdf/competitiveness2001.pdf (accessed October 2007).

15. The National Commission on Excellence in Education, *A Nation at Risk: The Imperative for Educational Reform*, submitted to U.S. Secretary of Education T. H. Bell on April 26, 1983. http://www.ed.gov/pubs/NatAtRisk/letter.html (accessed October 2007).

16. An excellent document on this topic, endorsed by CEAI and several dozen other professional organizations across a wide spectrum, is "Finding Common Ground," available for download from The First Amendment Center, www.first amendmentcenter.org.

17. "Mary Kay Letourneau," at Wikipedia.org. http://en.wikipedia.org/wiki/Mary_Kay_ Letourneau (accessed October 2007).

18. "Ex-Biology Teacher Gets Two Years for Sex with Student," *North Country Gazette*, October 5, 2006. http://www.northcountrygazette.org/articles/100506BirdsAnd Bees.html (accessed October 2007).

19. U.S. Census Bureau's American Fact Finder, "S1401: School Enrollment 2006." http://factfinder.census.gov/servlet/STTable?_bm=y&-geo_id=01000US&- qr_name=ACS_2006_EST_G00_S1401&-ds_name=ACS_2006_EST_G00_&- redoLog=false (accessed October 2007).

20. U.S. Census Bureau's American Fact Finder, "QT-P19: School Enrollment 2000." http://factfinder.census.gov/servlet/QTTable?_bm=y&-geo_id=01000US&- qr_name=DEC_2000_SF3_U_QTP19&-ds_name=DEC_2000_SF3_U (accessed October 2007).

21. Robert D. Putnam, *Bowling Alone: The Collapse and Revival of American Community* (New York: Simon & Schuster, 2000), pp. 299-300.

CHAPTER 3

What the Bible Says About Education

If you're looking for a Bible verse that tells you which education system to choose for your child, you'll be hunting for a long time. The Bible doesn't talk about public schooling versus private schooling versus homeschooling. In fact, it hardly talks about *schools* at all. Only once, in Acts 19:9, does it mention in passing that the apostle Paul borrowed somebody's "school" (*NASB*—other translations, including the *NIV*, say "lecture hall") for his meetings in Ephesus. So, no help there.

Neither will you find the words "education" or "educate" in Holy Writ. The times in which the Bible was written were not big on formal, ring-the-bell, do-the-curriculum learning.

This does not mean, however, that God does not care about the training and shaping of our minds or our children's minds. Far from it. Of the many Scriptures we could cite in both Old and New Testaments, perhaps the best place to start is at "the beginning of knowledge," as Proverbs 1:9 calls it. What is this starting point? "The fear of the Lord." That is the foundation on which all learning, all knowledge-gathering, all schooling should be built.

A few chapters later, a parallel proverb appears: "The fear of the Lord is the beginning of wisdom" (9:10).

For many people, these two sayings have become so familiar as to be clichéd. *Yes, of course—"the fear of the Lord"—whatever that means.* Many of us haven't actually made a connection between this concept and the day-to-day educational lives of our children.

What is the fear of the Lord, anyway? We pride ourselves as modern people on being courageous, in charge, unintimidated by others . . . fearless. We shy away from admitting we're fearful of anyone. *Can't scare me!* That's our chant.

So what brand of fear is this proverb talking about? Is this just a colorful way of telling us to treat God respectfully, because He's really a Nice Guy who wants everybody to be happy? After all, definitions of "fear" can run the gamut from "casual respect" all the way to "shaking-in-your-boots panic" at the towering presence of the One whose eyes are like fire. When God showed Himself to the elderly apostle named John on the Isle of Patmos, John reported that he "fell at his feet as though dead" (Rev. 1:17). Most of us would prefer to read about such dramatic encounters rather than have one.

At the Pritchard house, the two of us have come to believe that the fear of the Lord compels us always to be asking, "What does God think about this? What's His take on the matter?" After all, He loves our children even more than we do. They are His, in fact, and we are merely stewards for a season of these precious gifts. Surely we must consult His viewpoint on a subject as vital as their education, and continue to do so.

In other words, this "fear of the Lord" business is not just an arcane bit of theology to be discussed on Sundays. It has direct relevance to the school week, and we seek to take it seriously with regard to our children's education.

The part about *wisdom* originating in the fear of the Lord is important here as well. Wisdom is more than just information, as in "two plus two equals four" or "Abraham Lincoln was our sixteenth president." Wisdom is what guides us to use information toward good ends. Without a fundamental understanding of and regard for God, we can end up using information to do evil, rather than good.

It is sobering to note that Enron Corporation's chairman and CEO, who was convicted for his role in the biggest fraud scandal ever to hit American business, grew up the son of a Baptist preacher. Somewhere along the line, he apparently stopped asking, "What does God think?" In his quest for money, power, a Ph.D. and Washington connections, the fear of the Lord was left behind, and wisdom was only a distant memory.

We run the same risk if we attempt to manage our children's education without staying in touch with God's values and direction.

Teaching Kids to Fear? Yes!

As much as we all want to raise confident, self-reliant kids, there is no getting around the fact that the book of Deuteronomy calls us again and again to build a godly fear into our offspring, and ourselves as well. Listen to this drumbeat:

> Remember the day you stood before the LORD your God at Horeb, when the LORD said to me [Moses], "Assemble the people to Me, that I may let them hear My words so they may *learn to fear Me* all the days they live on the earth, and that they may teach their children" (4:10, *NASB*, emphasis added).

> You shall eat in the presence of the LORD your God, at the place where He chooses to establish His name, the tithe of your grain, your new wine, your oil, and the firstborn of your herd and your flock, so that you may *learn to fear the LORD your God always* (14:23, *NASB*, emphasis added).

When he [a future king] sits on the throne of his kingdom, he shall write for himself a copy of this law on a scroll in the presence of the Levitical priests. It shall be with him and he shall read it all the days of his life, that he may *learn to fear the* LORD *his God* (17:18-19, *NASB*, emphasis added).

Assemble the people, the men and the women and children and the alien who is in your town, so that they may *hear and learn and fear the* LORD *your God,* and be careful to observe all the words of this law. Their children, who have not known, will *hear and learn to fear the* LORD *your God,* as long as you live on the land which you are about to cross the Jordan to possess (31:12-13, *NASB*, emphasis added).

If that language seems too harsh, you may prefer the *New International Version*, which speaks of the need to "learn to *revere*" the Lord your God. Either way, this is an "acquired sensitivity." Fear or reverence of the Lord is something you may or may not have innately, but you can *learn* it. So can your children. Over time, as we hear God's voice, absorb His written Word and practice what it says, our attention to His point of view grows stronger. When contemplating an action that would be crosswise of His will, we sense an internal check. We think, *God wouldn't exactly endorse that, would He?* We stop and reconsider our course because we have *learned* to fear the Lord.

How does all this apply to education?

Fearing God When Choosing a Track

It's common these days for young churchgoing parents to approach us with the question, "Our son, Michael, is going to turn four next month, and we're already thinking about what kind of school he should go to. What do you think we should do?"

"Well," we reply, "have you prayed about it?"

"Oh, yes," they quickly respond, and then keep right on talking about human criteria. "But you know, we read in the paper that the test scores for District Such-and-Such are down 3 percent this year—and we're trying to see how we could afford Christian school tuition, but that's kind of steep, you know? We really need your guidance."

"Actually, the guidance you need," we say with a gentle tone, "is not so much from us as from the Lord. Ask Him what He wants you to do with Michael—and don't assume the answer based on some research report you read in the newspaper or online. Find out what God thinks."

We're not trying to be evasive here. And we're not trying to sound super-spiritual. We honestly believe that if God knows every detail of our lives down to the number of hairs on our child's head, He would not be aloof to a question as important as where that child should receive instruction.

When young parents push back and say, "Well, how would God ever answer that kind of prayer?" we reply, "Don't worry about it. God is big enough to figure out a method! You just do the asking. Let Him know that you really want to hear His take on the matter, and then watch what happens."

One young mom (whose husband works in full-time Christian ministry, no less) began reciting a flood of statistics she had read: "Well, I found out that if your children go to college and graduate with a bachelor's degree, their future income will be X. If they get a master's, it's estimated to be Y. And if they go on for a doctorate, it will be Z. So, the thing is, you've got to get them into the right colleges, which means going to the right high school and grade school, which means you've got to start with the right preschool . . ." It was all boiling down to a scientific formula. Pros versus cons. Statistics and probabilities. We felt like we were listening to somebody lay out their research for buying the best SUV or the best home theater system.

There's nothing wrong with research. Schooling decisions should not be made flippantly. But research and numbers are not the *beginning* of wisdom, according to God's Word. We need to start out by investigating soberly, reverently, even fearfully, what God thinks. This is where true knowledge begins.

It is easy to give lip service to the fear of the Lord while, in fact, acting based on a fear of people: *Which school has the fewest disciplinary problems? What if I have to admit to my friends that my kid didn't make it into a first-tier college? What if future employers aren't impressed by my child's transcript?* Such questions are all predicated on what people will think, and how our reputation as parents will stand up to scrutiny. It is as if we think we'll be judged based on what the world believes is important.

But the opinions of others are not nearly as important as the opinion of the heavenly Father.

Back in 1988, as our firstborn, Alyse, approached kindergarten age, we were typical young parents who wanted the best of everything for our precious daughter. We had already researched early-enrichment programs, from James Dobson books and videos to *How to Multiply Your Baby's Intelligence* by Glenn Doman—and a number of others. We read all kinds of books and articles. We monitored what was "hot" at the time. We certainly didn't want to blow it. We feared getting Alyse off onto the wrong foot by making a mistake when it came to her schooling.

Education had always been a big deal to the Pritchard family. In fact, that was one of the reasons David's father and his young bride moved more than 5,000 miles across the ocean from Samoa back in 1950. They wanted a quality learning environment for their yet-to-be-born children.

Making the right decision for Alyse seemed just as momentous. Centralia, Washington, where we lived at that time, had a strong Christian school as well as a large homeschooling network. We received a lot of friendly lobbying by people we knew and respected in both camps.

Kelli, with an education degree, was entirely ready to homeschool. She felt confident; she knew she could handle the job. And she loved our kids intensely. She was definitely not the kind of mom who was eager to push her child off the doorstep toward some school so that she could regain her "freedom." Spending the next two decades teaching Alyse and the others at home would have been Kelli's idea of paradise.

The flexible schedule that comes with homeschooling was a real plus in our minds, as well. It would have enhanced our lifestyle as small-business operators who were also involved as volunteers in a teen ministry.

But we didn't jump for any one option right away. We interviewed our pastor, seeking godly counsel. We talked with both sets of our parents, wanting to "honor your father and mother," as the Scripture says. After all, this was their grandchild. We met with principals and teachers we knew and asked lots of questions.

Most important, we sought the Lord. "God, we want Alyse to be where You think she should be," we prayed night after night. "Where is that? What are You thinking about this situation?"

The longer we prayed, the more we felt a nudge in the direction of public school. It was nothing external or dramatic; we simply sensed in our spirits that we should begin this route. Neither one of us considered that the die had been cast for her whole education, nor for all our kids yet to come. We said we would take it year by year, child by child, and see if God continued to affirm this choice.

In fact, sending Alyse to public school was the right choice. Her kindergarten teacher, who happened to be a Christian believer, was an excellent educator. We watched our daughter grow and blossom in her classroom. We began to understand the many things public school could do for her. We also saw aspects that needed our monitoring and even occasional intervention. But by the next year, we had decided that Alyse would continue her public-school career and sent her to first grade. The following year Krista started there as well, and then our son Tavita a year after that. We sensed God's confirmation each step of the way.

And the rest is history.

Fearing God More Than Textbooks

The fear of the Lord can guide us not only at enrollment time but also all through the school year—if we remember that His opinion counts. When surprises happen in our children's lives, when issues pop up and we don't know quite what to do or say, it is good to take a deep breath and imagine God taking in the whole scene, even as we consider what to do next.

What He thinks is a bigger deal than what any teacher or textbook says. We have often said to our kids, "Just because a teacher declares something or a textbook states something, doesn't mean it is part of Truth with a capital *T*. It may be, but it may not. There is only one True Book in this family. The Bible is the filter for everything else in our lives."

This does *not* mean that a kid has license to shoot off his mouth disrespectfully to a teacher about her words or her materials. Instead, we say, "We want you to engage your mind. We want you to think and evaluate everything you hear at school against what has been trained into your heart." Our prayer as parents is that the truth is so deep within them that anything divergent sticks out right away.

One day when Tana was in sixth grade, he came home with a language arts packet a student teacher had given out entitled "Fairy Tales." Kelli looked through it, as is her normal habit. All the kids know that Mom will quickly browse through their various materials, passing along to Dad anything of interest for his review as well.

Kelli came to a segment in the packet headlined "Religious Fairy Tales." *Hmmm . . . this is interesting,* she said to herself. *Let's see what's in here.*

Wouldn't you know, the very first story in the set was "Noah and the Ark."

Kelli stiffened immediately. "Tana, did you see this?"

"Yeah, Mom—I already spotted the Noah thing," he replied through a mouthful of after-school snack. "I'm going to talk to her about it tomorrow after class." He was five steps ahead of his mother.

Kelli took the opportunity to help him frame his comments. Together they developed what to say, something along the lines of "You know, it was interesting to see what's in the Religious Fairy Tales section. Actually, our family believes that the Noah event happened in real time and space. In fact, there's now even some archaeological evidence that supports this. I thought I'd just mention that there is another point of view."

Please note that we did not set Tana up to say, "You're wrong! What are you, an atheist? Don't you believe the Bible?! This stuff is trash!"

Nor did we pull him out of the class. Instead, we calmly and respectfully presented our viewpoint, couched in the framework of "Our family believes . . ." Who can argue against that? Everyone in America these days has the right to her own opinion, right? If some Internet junkie claims that telemarketers have a secret directory of cell phone numbers nationwide or that a particular brand of lipstick contains dangerous levels of lead, society nods and says that person is entitled to his personal opinion. For the Pritchards to believe in real animals inside a real ark riding out a real flood—well, that's their prerogative!

When Tana came home from school the next day, Kelli asked, "So how did it go in English class?"

"Mom, she was so embarrassed!" he reported. "She said she didn't even know that part was in the handout packet. She apologized all over the place for going against our family's beliefs. And she said she would go back and review the whole unit."

This was more than we had hoped for. We had only embraced the biblical account for our own sake, and it ended up affecting what 30 other kids in the class were taught as well.

On another day, Alyse's American History textbook turned up with a cleverly censored version of the Mayflower Compact, the governing document that the Pilgrims worked out just before landing at Plymouth Rock. It so happened that David had taught a Sunday morning class on this topic using materials from Dr. Marshall Foster of The Mayflower Institute, which had alerted us to watch for things like this—we were prepared with the original wording.

Instead of quoting the full first line of the Compact, which is "In ye name of God, Amen. We whose names are underwriten," and so forth, the textbook read:

> In ye name of . . . , Amen. We whose names are underwriten, the loyall subjects of our dread soveraigne Lord King James . . .

"Do you see these three dots at the start of the quote?" David asked the kids. "That's called an *ellipsis*. It shows that something has been left out. Would you like to know what it is?"

They were curious, of course.

He pulled out his class notes and showed the censored word: "In ye name of *God*, Amen." Their eyes grew wide as they looked at the textbook page.

"Now here is the real question," David continued. "Why do you think the textbook authors omitted that one word? What does that tell you about their views? Their biases?"

"It shows that they don't want to talk about God," said one of the kids.

"That's right. They want to skip around that topic. Let's look here in the front of your textbook and see who wrote this, where they went to school, what their background is." From this flowed an energetic interchange about academic integrity as well as alleged "separation of church and state."

Some people might say this story shows why Christian kids shouldn't be in public schools. We see it the opposite way. We see it as a great place to train kids in discernment. They find out who is being intellectually honest and who is not. They go back to school the next day with a juicy mystery to share with their class-mates: "Psst! Hey, you see these three dots here in the book? Wanna know what *didn't* get printed that's actually supposed to be there?"

We are not afraid of these things. We are far more afraid of failing to revere God in this situation.

This kind of exercise prepares students for bigger challenges to come. Our son Tavita, who is now at Stanford University, tells us that he commonly sits in a classroom where the professor up front actually *wrote* the textbook! So the book's opinion and the teacher's are identical. This is enough to intimidate any 19-year-old student, and it means Tavita has to be all the more prepared to filter things for himself.

Frequently, worried parents come to us saying, "You won't believe the latest thing that just happened at my kid's school. It's awful!" They launch into a passionate recounting of the inci-dent and then ask, "Should I pull my child out?"

"No," we reply. "What a great opportunity to teach your child what is truth and what is error! The situation itself is not nearly as important as what your child takes away from that situation.

The first task for you is to bolster your child's comprehension of God's reality. That's far more important than running over to 'fix' whatever the school is doing badly."

William Barclay, the Scottish scholar known for his easy-to-read commentaries, wrote in his book *Train Up a Child:*

> The New Testament knows nothing about religious education and nothing about schools, for the New Testament is certain that the only training which really matters is given within the home, and that there are no teachers so effective for good or evil as parents are.[1]

God has given us minds to use for His purposes. We must be good stewards by processing everything through His grid and teaching our children to do the same. Someday they will be doing this kind of work with the next generation. This is how the torch of faithfulness is passed down the line.

Fearing the Lord Where It Really Matters

We fully admit that not every public-school curriculum is manageable in the same way. Once in a great while, we have had to withdraw our children altogether from a set of lessons, most notably the middle school unit on puberty and human reproduction. Not because the information was false, but because it was incomplete without the moral dimension—and also because it would have had a desensitizing impact on our kids. Embracing privacy and modesty is a natural reaction for children when it comes to the topic of the human body, but once you destroy that response, there's no going back.

Our district requires that parents be notified when the human sexuality unit comes up and be given a chance to review the curriculum in advance. We've gone in to look it over. In the end, we have felt that it was far too clinical, so we have exercised our "opt-out" rights and had our children go to study hall instead. Meanwhile, we've been ready with our own Christian-based curriculum to cover with them at home (more about this in chapter 11).

Teachers have actually called to lobby us to allow our kids to take the course. "Are you sure you can't just keep Jordan in my class? She's got such a good mind, and she expresses herself so intelligently. I'd love to have her viewpoint in the class discussion."

"Well, thank you for the compliment," we respond. "We're glad she is proving to be a good student for you. But on this particular topic, we prefer to take our own approach. We're not saying the whole district ought to conform to our standards, but we do want to handle the sexuality issue in a way that honors our core beliefs. Please don't be offended by that."

"Okay, if that is your decision as parents, I will respect that. But I'll miss her!"

Some readers may disagree with us in this instance, saying that we're overreacting. Yes, we put our kids in the awkward position of having to stand alone from the group. But someday they'll truly have to stand alone when sexual temptation beckons. They might as well get used to being strong-minded and independent in this area of life.

We parents are accountable to God. We have to answer to Him about how we raise these children. We would rather err on the side of caution in such a high-octane area as sexuality.

Whether sidestepping a particularly unacceptable piece of instruction or, as is usually the case, working with the curriculum day by day, we cling to our eternal base of wisdom and knowledge: the fear of the Lord. We want this criterion to rule always in our hearts and in those of our kids as well: *What does God think of this? I sure don't want to irritate* Him!

When our older kids come home from college these days and sit around talking with us late at night, they sometimes reflect on their earlier years. They say things such as, "It's crazy how I never felt tempted by . . ." and name a certain drug or maybe a sinful behavior. "I was just too aware of what God would think about that."

To us parents, it's a rewarding moment. It tells us that the fear of the Lord lives inside them. This is what we have fervently hoped and prayed for all along the way.

When we first moved here to Lakewood (a southern suburb of Tacoma) in the summer of 2001, Alyse was heading into her senior year of high school, while Krista would be a sophomore. Having to move in the middle of high school was not popular with either of them, of course. But they bravely accepted the necessity.

That fall, we led a retreat at a camp as part of the Young Life ministry. Both Alyse and Krista attended and brought along some new friends from school. When we got home Sunday night, they told us, "Okay, now we know why we're here. Spending a weekend in a cabin with these girls and going through the talk sessions with our counselor—Mom and Dad, you wouldn't believe the brokenness in their lives. It was incredible. Some of them said they would never even have gone on this retreat if they hadn't gotten to know us first at school."

For the first time in their adolescent existence, some of these girls had encountered a different way of thinking. It was just starting to dawn on them that there really is a God who knows a ton more about life and reality than they ever thought. They realized that they needed to listen to Him after all. A scary idea, perhaps. But a good one at the same time.

Anchoring students' lives in the fear of the Lord is truly "the beginning of wisdom."

Note
1. William Barclay, *Train Up a Child: Educational Ideals in the Ancient World* (Philadelphia, PA: Westminster, 1959), p. 236.

CHAPTER 4

The Most Important Thing to Teach Your Public-School Child

Preparation for a new school year each August is a major job for every parent. Notebooks. Pens. Calculators. A cool-looking backpack. The "right" clothes. The "right" shoes. Or in some districts, uniforms mandated by school policy. A gym bag. Money for a lunch pass. Next-of-kin identification forms, complete with multiple work and cell phone numbers for contact at any hour in case of emergency. Proof of vaccinations. Proof of sports physical from the doctor's office. The list goes on and on.

If you send your child to a public school, you need to arm her with something more, however. The most important thing is not on sale at Target or Costco. The registration people won't ask for it, but you dare not leave it out.

The most important thing to teach your child is what Jesus (quoting Moses) said was the greatest commandment of all:

> Love the Lord your God with all your heart, and with all your soul, and with all your mind, and with all your strength (Mark 12:30).

Nothing is more important. Nothing is more foundational. Nothing will steer your child more effectively through the complexities, distractions and temptations of a day at public school. Young people who, of their own free will, deeply love the Lord and care about God's divine perspective can navigate the most treacherous waters with steady confidence.

We are talking about far more than just being a regular church kid. Lots of grade-school, middle-school and high-school students go through the Sunday motions, spend a week at summer camp, sing in the Christmas program, bring a can of green beans to the food drive and maybe even recite the Sinner's Prayer at some point along the way—but the core of their being is not captured by the love of God. Jesus asks for something far deeper.

We can tell this by the effusive way the sentence is worded. It doesn't just say, "Love God." It says to love Him with *all* your heart and *all* your soul and *all* your mind and *all* your strength. Nothing is halfway here. Jesus is talking about a total, all-encompassing embrace of the One who loves each of us more than we can ever comprehend.

All Your Heart

We Christian parents are not interested in raising little robots who can spout off a list of dos and don'ts—if that is all we achieve, the minute some situation pops up that doesn't fit the list, our child will drift and flounder. We are instead in pursuit of their *heart*. The heart is the center of the emotions. It is where the deepest loyalties reside. We want our child's heart so bonded to Christ that it can't stand the pain of separation.

It is not enough to expect right behavior from our child. We must expect right behavior with a right heart, a willing heart, a yielded heart. In other words, right behavior with a wrong heart is still wrong behavior. Doing the proper thing with a grudging attitude counts for nothing. Only when your child's heart is captivated by God will his behavior at school (and elsewhere) fall into line.

Does this sound impossible? Let us assure you it is not. Don't buy the lie of what society is saying about today's kids.

Don't accept that kids are just naturally disrespectful and surly these days. If you accept that as reality, then you will not parent them in a way that achieves anything different.

You *can* raise children and teenagers who respect you, respect other adults and respect God. You *can* see your sons and daughters grow increasingly closer to you and to God as the years go by, rather than hardened and disinterested. But first you must believe that it is possible.

We will get into the nuts and bolts of this process later in the chapter. But for now, let's take note of a vital cornerstone for building: *We* must evidence our own attachment to God "with all our heart."

Do your kids see in you a passion for pleasing the Lord? Do they sense that God is the most precious Person in your life? Do they know that you would never consciously displease Him? Watching how you live out your love for the Lord is how they will learn to love the Lord wholeheartedly.

All Your Soul

Closely related to loving God with our whole heart is loving God with our entire soul. (These four phrases, by the way, are not separate boxes on a table, distinct from one another. They are all intertwined in ways none of us fully comprehend.)

"Soul" is an interesting and somewhat perplexing word. We know it refers in some way to our eternal being, the part of us that lives forever—the part of us that survives the death of the body. The bumper sticker that reads, "He who dies with the most toys wins" is blatantly false. There's a better one out now that says, "He who dies with the most toys still dies!" Our society has always struggled to get the right perspective on material prosperity. We live in the most affluent economy in the history of the world, yet here in the United States depression is rampant, suicide is common and the misuse of prescription drugs is sky-rocketing—in other words, our *souls* are sick. People arrive at the twilight of their years and realize too late that they spent their entire lives chasing a phantom. Jesus said, "What good will it be for you to gain the whole world, yet forfeit your soul? Or what can you give in exchange for your soul?" (Matt. 16:26, *TNIV*).

The eternal destiny of every parent and every child is too important to assume that God will welcome us all into His heaven one way or another. Don't consign this crucial matter to the church, the youth pastor, the parachurch ministry to students (like Young Life, with whom we happen to work), or some evangelist on television. Make sure a salvation decision is made by every person under your roof, because it is truly a matter of life or death.

All Your Mind

One of the most important armaments you must give your children as you send them out the door to the public school is a relationship with God that fills all their minds. If the foundation of their faith rests on the good feelings they have while standing next to you in church, they are in trouble. If they don't know in their mind why they love God, if they are not "prepared to give an answer to everyone who asks [them] to give the reason for the hope that [they] have," and to "do this with gentleness and respect" (1 Pet. 3:15-16), they will be sitting ducks for any antagonistic teacher. When teachers and classmates ridicule anyone who has the audacity to believe in a sovereign, loving God, your kids won't know what to do or say.

What chance does a kid have against an "expert" unless that kid knows in his mind what he believes and why he believes it? It is not enough to counter with "My mom and dad said so."

The older your child gets in the public-school system, the more important this becomes. Certainly by middle school, the challenges to your child's faith will begin to come fast and furious, and will only intensify in high school. Then some evening you'll be sitting at the kitchen table with your son or daughter, looking over the slate of possible courses at university the next year—courses with titles like "The Problem of God" or "Perspectives on Science, Faith and Reality." You will sense by the way the course descriptions are written that some of these professors are just licking their chops in anticipation of exploding the "foolish myths" the next class of naïve freshmen will bring along from home.

Only the son or daughter whose mind has been stocked with what God thinks—and who has come to love those reliable, unshakable truths—will be prepared "so that when the day of evil comes, you may be able to stand your ground, and after you have done everything, to stand . . . with the belt of truth buckled around your waist" (Eph. 6:13-14). The love of God will be not only emotional and relational but also logical and intellectual.

Love is not merely a warm, fuzzy feeling associated mainly with Valentine's Day. Think about it: Our love for our spouse encompasses far more than that. We love the person we married for reasons of the mind as well as the heart. We are convinced that this person is the right partner for us—in fact, we made a conscious, well-considered, "left-brain" decision to live the rest of our earthly life with our spouse. So, to *"love* with all the *mind"* is not a contradiction in terms; rather, the mind enhances love, making it real, something of substance.

All Your Strength

What does it mean to love God with all our strength? If the first image that pops into your brain is Hercules with bulging muscles, put that aside. Instead, think about a high-school football game under the lights on a Friday night. Three quarters have been played—the fourth and final is about to start. If you're watching the Clover Park Warriors (the team I help coach), you'll see my players holding up four fingers as they stride toward the scrimmage line. By this, they're not trying to advise the clock operator. They are instead signaling to themselves and their teammates—*This is it! Fourth quarter! Here we go—give it everything you've got.* Even though they're tired, even though they might be a little dinged up, now is the time to dig down deep and fight with every remaining ounce of strength.

As we coaches often say, "Leave it all out on the field." Don't bring one iota of energy back to the bench when the final horn blows. Make us have to carry you to the locker room if necessary.

This kind of endurance is a picture of what it means to love God with all your strength. We want our kids to love God when it feels right, when things are going well—but also when life stinks. We don't want the Sunday "high" to fade out by Wednesday or Thursday. We want our children to love God through it all, straight on through the weekend, the semester, the week of final exams and every other challenge that comes their way.

The Bible says, "Let us not become weary in doing good, for at the proper time we will reap a harvest if we do not give up" (Gal. 6:9). This is a crucial part of loving God.

How Do We Measure?

By this point you may be saying, "It sounds good, of course— but how can I actually know that my child is loving God with all his heart, soul, mind and strength? It's too hazy. If I ask him whether he loves God, he will just give me the 'right answer.' There's no yardstick for this Great Commandment, is there?"

You are correct. This isn't something you can measure the way you test a kid's knowledge of multiplication tables or state capitals.

And yet, when you think about your child, you could prob-ably write a list of who and what your child loves, couldn't you? She loves Grandma . . . the family beagle . . . her cousin Stephanie . . . anything in the color pink . . . strawberry-kiwi smoothies . . . her art teacher at school.

Would you say God is on that list . . . or not? As parents, we know our child well enough to assess whether God is among the most cherished people in their life.

You've no doubt heard speakers ask, "If you got arrested for being a Christian, would there be enough evidence to convict you?" As clichéd as that might sound, there's a ring of truth in it. Each of us—adults as well as young people—must ask our-selves that question and think about how our day-to-day life would show what and who we truly love.

A wonderful story came out of Vietnam a few years ago about three peasant women who had been arrested because it had been discovered that they were Christian. The police held them in the local jail and kept trying to get them to con-fess to various crimes. Would they agree to plead guilty to "sedition against the state"? No, they insisted they had not offended the government. What about "inciting public disor-der"? No, their activities had always been peaceful. Time and again, the three women kept dodging what the police wanted them to confess.

Finally, a resolution was found. The trio agreed to accept this charge: "These women love God more than normal." A pun-ishment was then meted out to them.

Let it be said about ourselves and our children here in free North America, that *we love God more than is normal.* Our deci-sions and choices are governed not by the popular "wisdom" of the day but instead by what we understand God intends for us. Clinging to Him in love will serve us well both here and in the world to come.

From Theory to Practice

Now that we understand the goal, what are the steps that will get our families there? What do we need to do on a regular basis to nurture this all-out love for God in our children?

A good starting point is what God said to Moses immediately following the Great Commandment, as recorded in Deuteronomy 6. Right after the sentence that says to "Love the Lord your God with all your heart . . ." come these words:

> These commandments that I give you today are to be upon your hearts. Impress them on your children. Talk about them when you sit at home and when you walk along the road, when you lie down and when you get up. Tie them as symbols on your hands and bind them on your foreheads. Write them on the doorframes of your houses and on your gates (vv. 6-9).

This passage is in fact the Jewish confession of faith, recited weekly in synagogues. It has great significance for Christians as well, as it calls us to *infuse daily life* with discussion about God's truth. What we adults claim to believe and cherish needs to become *visual* and *verbal*, or kids will never know. They can only grasp what they see and hear from us.

In a minute we will describe for you what shape this takes at the Pritchard house. We don't want you to think this is the only way to do it—or that you have to imitate our method exactly. We aren't claiming to be perfect. Other Christian families are raising godly kids who thrive in public school through different means. But each of those families is doing something *intentional*. They aren't just assuming that their kids will gain a solid faith by osmosis. They know, as Deuteronomy implies, that parental initiative is essential.

Having said that, here is what we've developed for our eight kids:

Every school morning of the week, we gather in our family room at 6:30 A.M. in our pajamas to start the day with Bible reading—specifically, the books of Psalms and Proverbs. Many years ago we heard about Billy Graham's personal habit of reading five psalms and one chapter of Proverbs each day, thus completing both books once a month (there are 150 short psalms, and Proverbs has 31 chapters—so the math works out nicely). We decided long ago to borrow his idea for our devotion time with our growing family, and we've kept it going ever since.

The book of Psalms is all about our relationship with God, while the book of Proverbs is all about our relationship with humanity. Put them together, and you have the necessary wisdom for conducting your life, both vertically and horizontally. No, these two don't cover everything God has revealed to us, and we encourage ourselves and our kids to study the other 64 books of the Bible on our own. We naturally hear sermons and attend Sunday classes at our church that focus on other books. But together as a family, we concentrate on mining the tremendous wealth of Psalms and Proverbs.

At the time we started, Alyse (our oldest) was just in first grade, but we had also taken in three high-school boys who needed a stable home for a season, and we desperately wanted to plant some of God's Word in their hearts. We made the decision simply to read God's Word and let it speak to us all. We began seeing the fruit of that, and have kept seeing it all through the years.

Yes, it's hard to get everybody awake and downstairs at 6:30 in the morning! Kids show up on chilly mornings wrapped in blankets and still rubbing their eyes. But think about it: The day has to get started sooner or later anyway. We might as well be definite about it. Six-thirty is the "show your face" hour at our house on school days, no discussion or debate.

Our older college-aged kids tell us now that this commitment to get them up every morning to read the Bible together
made a huge impression on them. It told them what Dad and
Mom considered important—the beginning of knowledge, so
to speak. And it started their day, before their minds had been
cluttered with trivia, by focusing on God's reality.

During our morning devotions, we go around the circle
and each take turns reading a couple of stanzas or sections,
usually from the *New International Version*. We, Kelli and David,
listen for key concepts that tie in with things our kids are currently dealing with, events in the news and real situations that
people face. The Psalms in particular keep driving home the
point that God is bigger than our issues. He's bigger than the
public school. He's bigger than the worst thing going on this
week. Consider this soaring passage (which we get to read every
twenty-third day of the month):

> The LORD is exalted over all the nations, his glory
>   above the heavens.
> Who is like the LORD our God, the One who sits
>   enthroned on high,
> who stoops down to look on the heavens and the
>   earth? (Ps. 113:4-6).

Irrelevant to school life, you say? Think again. This passage
implants in a young person's mind who the ultimate authority
really is. It establishes the true "chain of command" in this
world. It also declares that the God of heavens is watching what
goes on here below. He's paying attention.

We talk about these truths as we read God's Word. And it
doesn't end there. After the Psalms, we hit Proverbs.

The book of Proverbs deals with intensely practical matters,
from money to laziness to sex to overeating to mouthiness.

We try not to assume the role of the Holy Spirit, by pressing these instructions on our kids; instead, we read the Scripture verses and let God make them relevant. It takes the focus off Dad and Mom so that our kids receive what is being read as *God's* wisdom, not ours. If they drop a comment along the lines of "That's not realistic" or "I don't like what that says," we can say, "Well, when you get to heaven, you can take that up with God!"

Every month when we get to the twenty-eighth day, Mom takes the lead for Psalm 136, her favorite. It's written in the form of a chant:

> **Kelli:** Give thanks to the Lord, for he is good.
>> **The rest of us:** *His love endures forever.*
>
> **Kelli:** Give thanks to the God of gods.
>> **The rest of us:** *His love endures forever.*
>
> **Kelli:** To the One who remembered us in our low estate
>> **The rest of us:** *His love endures forever.*
>
> **Kelli:** And freed us from our enemies
>> **The rest of us:** *His love endures forever* (vv. 1-2,
>> 23-24, emphasis added).

When we finish the psalm, we keep the chant going with our own current reasons to praise God:

> Our basketball team was awesome last night—
> *His love endures forever.*
>
> We get to go to the beach this Saturday—
> *His love endures forever.*

This practice supplies yet another building block in the biblical foundation we are erecting in our children's minds: an understanding that God is the Source of all good things in our lives.

There's even a creative way to deal with Psalm 119, the longest "chapter" in the Bible. What we do is save that one for the months that have a thirty-first day. Having finished the rest of the book on the thirtieth, we then give this final day of the month to reading Psalm 119 (along with Proverbs 31). Otherwise, we skip it.

But we certainly don't want to miss the gems of this particular section, such as:

> How can a young man keep his way pure?
> By living according to your word.
> I seek you with all my heart;
> do not let me stray from your commands.
> I have hidden your word in my heart
> that I might not sin against you. . . .
> Open my eyes that I may see
> Wonderful things in your law.
> I am a stranger on earth;
> do not hide your commands from me (Ps. 119:9-11,18-19).

Our morning Bible reading is different from a "Bible study," in which participants dissect a short passage of Scripture and explore its subtle meanings. We simply keep reading—and keep coming back next month and the next month and the month after that. The curious thing is that while the text remains constant, our life circumstances keep changing. Parents *and* kids keep growing up, with new experiences and fresh understanding. What Proverbs says about "discretion" means one thing to an 8-year-old (and perhaps has to be explained by a parent), while it strikes a 12-year-old differently. And once a kid hits 16, it has a wider meaning.

Does "familiarity breed contempt"? No. Actually, we find that the older kids enjoy our Bible readings more as the years go by. They look forward to verses they can finish by memory.

They also come up with new applications. More than once we've heard one of them say, "I don't remember that being in there!" In these *aha!* moments, the verse finally becomes the living Word of God to them.

None of us who call ourselves Christian should be arrogant to assume that just because we've read a certain passage in the past, we've now "got it." The power of the Bible is that it is evergreen, always speaking afresh to our condition.

Springing from this "evergreen" quality of God's Word is its unique ability to convey values and shape behavior. We heard about one missionary in Mongolia, of all places, who said that followers of Tibetan Buddhism there found Proverbs in particular appropriate for shaping the character of their young people. These Buddhists felt it would make their sons and daughters more responsible, self-disciplined and industrious in adulthood. The missionary said, "In this culture, I have come to believe that if the gospel is the Seed, the book of Proverbs is a useful plow to break up the hard soil, so the Seed can find a place to sprout and grow."

Along the way, we have realized a few great by-products of our morning custom. One is that it gives our kids great practice at reading out loud. We see right away how they're doing at recognizing words and enunciating them, without mumbling. If one of our kids needs help in this area, we catch it right away.

Another "perk" is the opportunity to build vocabulary. We have to stop and talk, for example, about what the word "prudent" means (our kids assumed at first that it was an adjective related to "prude" until we looked it up together!). When we hit terms such as "chaste" or "humility" or "perpetual," we make sure the meaning is clear to our kids. Kelli has a famous line at such moments: "This could show up on the SAT! We'd better find out what this word means!" Everybody goes, "Yeah, Mom," but their vocabularies are enhanced nevertheless.

Choose Your Own System

Again, we say that our method is not the only way to help your child "love God more than normal." But whatever system you choose, be diligent to follow through on this most important work in the lives of your children. The great French mathematician Pascal wrote about the "God-shaped vacuum in the heart of every man." There is a God-shaped vacuum in our brains as well. If we parents do not fill both with loving knowledge and passionate understanding of God, the outside world will be glad to fill them with lesser things.

As you nurture this vital love affair with God, we encourage you to turn frequently to the writings of David and the other psalmists. David was not perfect by any means. He messed up repeatedly, even as an adult who should have known better. But you have to admit, here was a man who *truly loved God*. His heart was directed toward the North Pole of God's greatness, despite an occasional wobble here and there. He wanted with all his being to please the Lord. Listen to his cry:

> O God, You are my God;
> Early will I seek You;
> My soul thirsts for You;
> My flesh longs for You
> In a dry and thirsty land
> Where there is no water (Ps. 63:1, *NKJV*).

We can't guarantee that the line "Early will I seek You" means 6:30 in the morning. But if, by whatever method, we all can build this kind of passion in our children, we will have given them the living water that they need in the "dry and thirsty land" of today's culture.

CHAPTER 5

The Second Most Important Thing...

The second most important thing to teach your public-school child is *to obey you unconditionally.*

"Well, of course that's a good idea for home life," you may say, "but what's the connection to school? I don't get it."

Here is the profound link you may never have thought about. The child who has been taught to obey Dad and Mom understands two very important truths about his or her life:

1. *I'm not the boss around here—somebody else is in charge of me.* This is not meant to demean the child's worth at all. Nobody is saying he is a piece of trash that can be wadded up and thrown across the room. We are simply saying that in the grand order of things, he is not the top dog, the "little emperor." The word "obedience" is actually getting a bad reputation in some circles these days. People say it sounds like domination or the squelching of a child's personality. "You shouldn't suppress your child," they claim. "If you train him to obey, he might end up yielding to some predator some day." Nonsense. That is not at all what obedience is about.

2. *My parents sometimes delegate their authority to other responsible people.* For example, parents go out for an evening and put a babysitter in charge. This means

the child has to obey the babysitter, who has been commissioned (to use the Latin phrase) in *loco parentis*—"in place of the parent." Our standard line with our kids on these evenings has always been, "Make it easy on the person in charge." This is an extremely important principle for the child to have in mind when she walks through the school door. The child who has a healthy and obedient relationship with her parents at home finds it quite natural to obey the teacher, the coach, the principal. She instinctively assumes that Mr. Johnson and Mrs. Englehart occupy the same kind of role as Dad or Mom. They are to be obeyed—end of discussion.

More and more parents these days, it seems, are uncertain about whether they should insist on obedience. They ask their child to hang up his coat or run an errand. The child ignores them, walks away or snaps back with, "Can't you see I'm busy?" And the parent just shrugs this off! *After all, it's just us here within the confines of home, so it's not a big deal. Maybe I'll deal with this kind of behavior next time,* they tell themselves.

But then the next morning the child goes to school. Is it any wonder that this same kid won't follow his teacher's directions? Inside his head he's saying, *Why should I have to do what the teacher says?*

Hello!? What makes us think that kids who disobey their parents at home are going to change when they hit the school threshold? Their ability to grasp anything the public school has to offer in terms of education has been derailed. The most basic classroom command, "Sit down, take out your book and turn to page 34," becomes an ordeal for the teacher to pull off.

"Classroom management" (the formal terminology used by educators) has become a huge burden these days. It requires an incredible amount of energy and time, pulling teachers away from their core purpose: to *teach*. Instead, they are bogged down with the constant necessity for "Quiet, please. Stop that. Quit bothering your neighbor. Pay attention."

Substitute teachers get the worst of it in today's environment. Too many undisciplined students walk in the room, take one look, see the "sub" and immediately begin plotting how to create bedlam.

In just one or two generations, things have changed dramatically. It used to be that kids who got into trouble at school would beg, "Please don't call my folks!" Today, students simply retort, "Lay off my case, or I'll get my folks to call our lawyer!" Down this road lies only chaos and deterioration for a society. And that won't help any of us. We have to find a way to turn this around.

Ten Steps Ahead

When you send a boy or girl out the door in the morning who already knows how to obey, that child is well on the road to doing well in public school. He or she is already 10 steps ahead of his or her peers. The ability to obey Dad and Mom transfers directly to the teacher.

The truth is, teachers unconsciously spend more time with and grant more favor to obedient students. They don't mean to, of course. They might even deny the fact, insisting that they "treat everyone alike." But human nature being what it is, teachers simply enjoy interacting with obedient kids.

Teachers have said to us, "David and Kelli, *please* stay here in the public school. Your kids are such a joy to teach. They're leaders for the rest. Please don't go anywhere else!"

On the other hand, I (David) can tell you straight out as an assistant football coach that *attitude directly affects opportunity*. If you send me a player who is late for practice half the time, argues or whines whenever I instruct him to run laps, won't memorize the playbook and won't get his weight down to where I tell him it should be, I guarantee that this is what his stats will look like at the end of the season:

- Minutes played   =4
- Carries handled   =2 (if he's lucky)
- Yards gained   =0
- Touchdowns scored   =0

That is just the reality of football for the kid who thinks he can play but doesn't want to obey the coaching staff.

Not much is being said or written these days in the popular press about how the breakdown of family structure and parenting skills negatively affect the educational process. But to us, it is a glaring reality. Here is a bold declaration that may irritate some readers: *If we parents don't provide the school with a student who is (a) awake, (b) alert, (c) fed and (d) cooperative, we have no right to complain about test scores.* The numbers generated by a classroom full of half-asleep, cranky kids with growling stomachs are going to be awful—how could we expect otherwise? Until we take back our responsibility to train our children in obedience, the teachers and schools will continue to be unfairly blamed for our kids' failure.

We parents must not embrace the cop-out: "Well, that's the school's job. They need to crack down, get tougher with those kids. Make 'em mind!"

No, it is not their job. Personally speaking, we do not want the Pritchard kids to be taught obedience by hired school personnel. Their job is to educate, not to form character. We will take care of that ourselves.

If by some miracle, every public-school student showed up to class tomorrow morning with an obedient spirit, American education would be instantly revolutionized.

So How Do We Accomplish This?

Obedience is in decline, we believe, because training takes time. You can't achieve results quickly, and daily reinforcement gets monotonous. It's labor-intensive. It can cost you sleep, relaxation time with your spouse and other things you enjoy.

But we have to take our job seriously, nonetheless.

I (Kelli) remember watching one preschooler challenge his mom, who murmured to me with a touch of embarrassment, "We haven't had time to deal with that yet."

I stood there with my mouth hanging open. *If you don't have time to deal with the obedience issue when the child is 3, what's going to happen when he's 6 . . . or 16?* I thought. What is cute at age 3 ("No! I won't go to bed!") is no longer cute in junior high.

It's like the old Fram oil filter commercial, in which the mechanic encourages consumers to spend a few dollars today to prevent engine failure in the future. He says, "You can pay me now, or you can pay me later." Parents can "change the filter" with a toddler, or they can replace the whole engine with a teenager.

Many parents today are, in fact, training their children to be *dis*obedient. That sounds crazy—but look at it from the child's perspective:

If my dad asks me to go out to the curb and drag back the empty garbage cans, I can ignore him the first time. I have better things to do.

I can ignore him the second time, too.

I can probably ignore him the third time.

When he raises his voice on the fourth time, I need to start paying attention.

Once he stands up, I've got to watch him closely.

When he actually begins walking toward me, I need to jump up and start doing what he asked me to do.

This child has learned by experience that the first five requests don't really count. Only on the sixth try does he have to obey.

The bigger issue here is selfishness. The child is learning that it is all right to tend to his own agenda first. What Dad is asking him to do is not a priority. The garbage cans can wait.

When parents say to us with frustration, "But what if I can't get them to do what I say the first time?" we reply, without meaning to oversimplify, "How do you get results the sixth time? Do that the first time instead." Take firm action right away, without the long build-up. Do this for a week or two, and your child will get the picture that a new day has dawned. In fact, kids will make the switch faster than the parents. They pick up right away that stalling around doesn't work anymore.

Deep down, obedience is a heart issue. That is why we said in the last chapter that doing the right thing with a negative heart is not good enough. We parents cannot afford to ignore the body language that often accompanies inner resistance: the stomping of feet, the slamming of doors, the rolling of eyes, the heavy sigh. This shows a lack of submission on the inside. We talk often in our family about doing things with "a happy heart." Anything less is simply "creative disobedience"—doing what you have to do in order to stay out of trouble, to keep your privileges, to get the car keys or whatever. But internally, you are still being defiant.

When this happens with our kids, we don't hesitate to say, "Wait a minute—let's back up and try that again. Rewind the tape." We give the instruction a second time and watch for full obedience with the right attitude.

A friend told us about his observation one time at the end of a school event when our Tana, who was then in seventh grade, asked permission to go with some friends to a house for some game time. David thought through the request and then said, "Well, no, that's not going to work, because neither Mom nor I can pick you up later on. We're both tied up." Tana just quietly said, "Okay." My friend complimented the way he handled his disappointment.

Well, this was the result of a long training process. Tana, in fact, is what many would call a "strong-willed child." He's not a pushover. But early on, we set in place the expectation for obedience. No eye rolls. No head shakes. We remember often saying, "Tana, wait a minute. Say 'Yes, Dad' or 'Yes, Mom' once more, but without the drama this time." This started back when he was three and four years old, so that today, when he's 6'2" and a starting quarterback on his football team, the pattern is well established.

His little brother, Keila, is our high-energy fifth-grader. At the time of this writing, he's having a bit of trouble remembering to pick up his lunch sack as he heads out the door in the morning. The rule in our house is that if you forget your lunch, you don't ask for it to be taxied to you at school and you don't borrow money from your friends to buy something. Instead, you go hungry. Your lunch will be waiting for you on the kitchen counter when you get home at three o'clock.

School staff members have a hard time with this! They will call us asking how to solve the problem. Can't they just give Keila a voucher to go through the lunch line, and we can pay it back later? We say, "No, he'll be all right. This is not a crisis. Hunger isn't going to kill him. He'll remember better next time."

If they protest further, we add, "You know, this is part of the reason why you *like* him as a student! We've trained him to accept the natural consequences of his disobedience. We're building character and endurance here. He'll be fine."

Keila comes home and cheerfully reports, "Mom, I told them not to bother calling you. I knew what you'd say. But they did it anyway—I didn't ask them to, honest! Now, where's my brown bag?"

A Divine Dimension

The matter of obedience is so central that it made it into the Ten Commandments: "Honor your father and your mother" (Exod. 20:12). Likewise, in the New Testament, it is one of the few clear instructions provided about family life. "Children, obey your parents in the Lord, for this is right" (Eph. 6:1; also see Col. 3:20).

God *didn't* say, "Make sure your children brush their teeth" or "Insist on nine hours of sleep each night." But He *did* say we are to teach our children how to obey. This is fundamental. It is not negotiable.

Actually, the call for obedience goes back all the way to the Garden of Eden. At the very dawn of human history, a woman and her husband disregarded the one rule their heavenly Father had laid down—and it turned out to be a very big deal. God did not say, "Oh, well—try to remember next time, okay?" No, He dealt with the disobedience head-on. We are still feeling the aftershocks of that moment.

What God was looking for in Eve and Adam is the same thing He wants from us: a humble spirit that submits willingly to His authority because we respect and love Him. It's not just obedience for obedience's sake. It is, rather, a response driven by what we've learned about His character and His wisdom. In this case, Father really does know best.

Nehemiah prayed to "the God of heaven, the great and awesome God, who keeps His covenant of love with those who love Him and obey His commands" (see Neh. 1:5, *NASB*). This Jewish leader held the highest regard for God, knowing that wonderful things come to those who comply with His instructions. John, the beloved disciple, wrote, "This is love for God: to obey his commands. And his commands are not burdensome, for everyone born of God overcomes the world" (1 John 5:3-4).

In the same way that our obeying God comes as a result of our relationship with Him, our children's obedience should spring from the richness of our connection with them. In various ways, we need to communicate why our kids should obey us: "You know our hearts. You know how much we love you. We've lived longer than you have, and made more mistakes. So now, we're trying to coach you to avoid some of the pain we've experienced along the way."

This is not at all like what the authoritarian says: "Look, kid, you have to obey me—the Bible says so!" Yes, it does—but the heart of our work as parents is to build an amazing love relationship with them so that obedience follows naturally.

Frustrated parents sometimes moan, "I can't get this kid to obey me!" Well, guess what—*that's exactly true*. You cannot force obedience once the child gets beyond the preschool years. You instead have to instill in him or her an internal desire to obey, based on the child's warm relationship with you as well as with God.

We've heard parents ask, "What if kids won't get up on Sunday morning and go to church?" That has never been an option at our house—the pattern has been set from infancy with each child. The kids know that going to church on Sunday is just what we do. But we don't drag them, either; that would just spawn more problems. Instead, we encourage our children to see church participation for what it truly is: an outpouring of our love and appreciation for God. It's a relational thing.

Obedience based on relationship is far more compelling than obedience based on "I'm the dad around here, and you *will* do what I say!" Remember that. If you put in the time now to build a loving relationship, you're investing in future obedience.

Let's be honest: Sooner is better than later for getting the real picture of where things stand between you and your child. If you avoid facing reality, it is likely to manifest itself when your child goes to school. That is when your child shows her true colors—and you'll know whether she's learned to obey, or not.

Don't train for obedience out of a desire for good reputation so that others will say, "Look at that well-behaved child. What a good mom she must be." Do it rather to convey to your child the bigger picture of how life works. Do it so that your child comes to enjoy the benefits of an ordered life. To follow the directions of a parent, a teacher, a boss and most of all, one's God, is to set the stage for a fruitful adulthood.

The bottom line is this: Our kids need to come under our authority. The ultimate objective is to acquire our child's buy-in to our family's beliefs, especially in the area of obedience. Otherwise, the teenaged years especially are going to be rough. In a sense, we are asking them to *voluntarily* place themselves under the authority of their less-than-competent parents.

A Dad's Role

Dads in particular have an assignment here. The Bible says, "Fathers, do not exasperate your children; instead, bring them up in the training and instruction of the Lord" (Eph. 6:4). This does not diminish the role that moms have in raising the kids, of course. But I (David) do find that for some reason, I hold a unique key to our kids' emotional state. They take a lot of their cues from me.

And it is my job to set the pace for their obedience *without* exasperating them. That is a hazard, I admit. Like many males, I tend to assess a situation quickly, come up with a solution and declare a plan of action—which, by the way, is the final answer and not up for debate! That can be terribly frustrating if my son or daughter feels I haven't taken all the factors into consideration. Maybe they have further information related to the case, and I didn't hear them out. Now they feel trapped.

The parallel Scripture in Colossians puts it this way: "Fathers, do not embitter your children, or they will become discouraged" (Col. 3:21). A child beaten down by a father's too-quick summary judgment is a sad thing to watch. Yes, we need to teach obedience, and we will not always win a popularity contest doing so. But we men also need to be aware of the times our kids are exasperated with us, and at least be willing to ask ourselves, *Why?*

The point is not simply to be tough or demanding. We must have no desire to be dictators. The point is rather to follow what God has said is best for kids both inside the home and out—particularly in places such as school.

Of course, God didn't give us a mandate to train up our children in obedience because parents are always right. We're definitely not. He commanded it because *somebody* has to be in charge of a household, and that somebody is the parent. The children God has given us will someday grow up to be in charge of their own families. They need a solid example of how to do that correctly, biblically, sensitively.

Finding the right balance between firmness and sensitivity can be tricky sometimes. We all err to one side on one day and the opposite on another. We don't always get it right. But we have to try. To do nothing is to default to the "soft" extreme.

One Saturday before Labor Day, our family was slated to go to a lake for a great half-day of swimming, water sports and picnicking. We had all looked forward to this for a long time. Throughout the morning before our departure, however, Jordan (then 13) and her younger brother Tana (10) kept snapping at each other. Both of them were in a feisty mood and kept giving each other grief.

We asked them a couple of times to knock it off and be nice. The squabbling continued.

What would be the standard consequence that most parents would use? Separating them from each other, of course.

We decided on the opposite. "Okay, you guys," we announced, "you two are going to stay home from the excursion to the lake. And here's the deal: *You have to stay right next to each other all weekend.* Whatever one does, the other has to be right there. You may not pull away from each other for any reason from now until Monday night, except for sleeping or going to the bathroom. Basically, you're Siamese twins. You have no choice but to get your interaction with each other straightened out."

They were disappointed to miss the fun at the beach, of course. Once we pulled out of the driveway, they stared at each other. Now what? They couldn't avoid each other, because they knew we'd be checking up when we got home.

So they went outside and shot baskets for a while. They got on the phone and called their grandmother for sympathy. They thought up other things to keep themselves busy (we had specified that they could not just veg in front of the TV for hours and hours).

When we got back home that evening, their relationship had definitely improved. They continued to have occasional flare-ups, but for the most part, they were getting the point that it was not an option in our house for two family members to be mean to each other.

More than once since then, we've overheard them saying to each other in the middle of a disagreement, "Okay, you know we have to work this out." The idea of having their parents get into the act again was definitely undesirable! They would much rather solve things themselves.

Playing Catch-Up

Parents have confessed to us, "I'm way late in starting all this. My child is now 12 years old (or 14 . . . or 16). I've really been soft on the obedience thing, and I'm seeing the ugly results. What do I do at this stage?"

We reply, "You sit down with your child and say, 'I'm sorry—please forgive me. I have not done what God asked me to do with you. I'm going to do better from now on. Here is what it's going to look like.' And then you start spelling out the details you've carefully drafted."

The speech to the child continues: "I'm going to mess up in the future, I'm sure. And you're going to mess up. So we're going to have to forgive each other. But it is now my expectation, as we go forward, that you will obey. Not just sometimes. Every time. I love you too much to keep failing you the way I've done in the past. So I *will* teach you to obey. This *is* going to happen."

We warn them that the kid will no doubt look into their eyes for some chink, some wavering, some crack of hesitation. But the son or daughter must find nothing to exploit—and leave the conversation persuaded that Dad or Mom has finally seen the light and is determined to follow it.

The payoff, after some initial anguish, will be huge. The joy of having fun together on a sure footing cannot be described. We honestly have to tell you that we are absolutely crazy about our kids. We can't wait for them to come home. And obedience is the foundation of that relationship.

School Rules

The apostle Paul complimented one group of Christians by writing, "You have always obeyed—not only in my presence, but now much more in my absence" (Phil. 2:12). This is what we are trying to achieve as parents, too.

We tell our kids, "Your operating instruction for school is this: Obey whatever you're told, unless it's flat-out illegal or immoral. That way, we can go to bat for you in questionable situations. If a teacher makes a big mistake and is unfair to you, we can stand up for you—because we'll know that your track record is otherwise clean."

In fact, we even teach our kids that when a classmate disobeys, it is not enough just to wait on the sidelines. They need to see if they can be part of the solution. That's called leadership. Granted, it is not always possible, and sometimes they just have to walk away. But opportunities do arise to speak into the difficulty. We've been pleased to hear secondhand from teachers about how various members of our family have been vocal with their acquaintances: "Come on, stop it, man. You don't need to be doing that."

If you fear that the tide of influence will run the other way—that public-school classmates will drag your child down from his or her standards—then this means you have some training yet to do. The foundation of obedience is perhaps a little flimsy. On the other hand, if you are truly raising a warrior for the Lord, you can let them excel even in the midst of opposition.

After all, your children are going to be exposed to the miscreants and troublemakers of the world anyway. There's no magic age at which your children become exempt from negative influence. You are in the business of raising *influencers* who will go out and make a difference in this society, wherever God places them.

Consistent obedience is not an impossible dream for your child. It is essential for him if he is to function and thrive in today's world. You can do it!

CHAPTER 6

The Third Most Important Thing...

Closely related to obedience is the third most important thing to teach your public-school child: *self-control.* The two are similar but not identical. Obedience is the response to an outside authority. Self-control, on the other hand, is internal and free-standing. It is how a young person behaves whether Mom or Dad is in same zip code, let alone the same room. The child has been trained to *tell himself* yes or no, based on certain criteria.

At birth, we parents hold virtually all the control; the infant is like clay in our hands. We give instruction and gradually transfer more and more decisions toward the child, so that by age 18 or so, he or she arrives at the point of total *self*-control, where we no longer have to exert outside pressure. The young person is now self-governing.

On a chart, it looks like this:

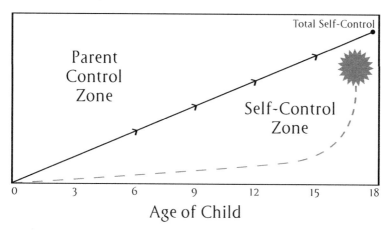

If we are afraid to enable self-control, and keep holding on to the reins until late in the game (see dotted line), we can end up causing an explosion of irresponsibility. When this happens, it is because our children are not prepared to control themselves. They don't know how to handle situations in which they have to call their own shots. They end up doing things that are foolish and sometimes outright dangerous.

All of the major challenges of growing up demand this vital quality called self-control. Managing your weight. Getting out of bed on time in the morning. Walking away from a playground fight. Not wasting your money. Keeping your hands where they belong on a date.

And *definitely* going to school.

The ability to focus in the classroom, to take in information in a steady stream, is essential. When any parent tells us their child is not doing well in school, one of the first questions we ask is, "How self-controlled would you say he is?" If this quality has not been ingrained in the first five years of the child's life, the kindergarten teacher (and all who follow her) is going to have a very tough time getting anything to stick.

To sit and read a chapter of American history takes self-control. To sit and listen to a teacher explain a math formula takes self-control. Educators are having a hard time these days with too many kids who arrive with no desire to sit, listen and comprehend; they instead want to be entertained. Most teachers weren't trained in the drama department and can't compete with MTV and video games.

There is a direct correlation between self-control and school performance at all grade levels. The self-controlled student says, "This project isn't due until next month—but I'm going to get moving on it now. I'll do a little at a time, so I don't have to crash the night before." The payoff for this way of thinking is great for the individual as well as for family peace. It fosters success throughout high school, college and even beyond.

In any less-than-ideal classroom, students with self-control will be better able to ignore distractions. They will keep focusing regardless. When somebody in the next desk wants to goof off, when somebody in the cafeteria wants to ditch school for the afternoon, when somebody in the locker room wants to sell drugs, the self-controlling person is not drawn off balance. He or she has what might be called an "internal policeman" calling silent signals, notifying the brain of what is in bounds and what is not.

More than 200 years ago, the esteemed British statesman Edmund Burke wrote:

> Men are qualified for civil liberty in exact proportion to their disposition to put moral chains upon their own appetites. . . . Society cannot exist unless a controlling power upon will and appetite be placed somewhere, and the less of it there is within, the more there must be without.[1]

When the "controlling power" is internal, you don't have to pay for so many cops on the street (or monitors in the school hallway). It is embarrassing to realize that America's prison population during just the past 30 years has multiplied *tenfold*, from approximately 200,000 to more than 2 million.[2] Taxpayers can hardly keep up with the need for more correctional cells, more squad cars and more detectives. All because *self-control* is in such short supply.

Dr. Jennifer Roback Morse, who formerly taught economics at both Yale and George Mason universities, is now a research fellow at Stanford's Hoover Institution. She and her husband also have two children (one adopted), plus foster kids from time to time. She writes:

A free society needs people with consciences who can control themselves and use their freedom without bothering other people too much. But no one develops a conscience and self-control in a social vacuum. Your marriage has the potential to create children who can strengthen a free society—or significantly weaken it.[3]

At the classroom level, this shortage of self-control sabotages the popular educational strategy called *collaborative learning*, which means kids work together on a project in small groups. This is one way teachers are seeking to keep today's students involved and paying attention.

But collaborative learning requires focusing on and working through the assignment as you sit together around a table. Our kids are constantly coming home saying, "Mom, I've been put in this group, and nobody else is doing any work! I'm going to have to do it all myself to get any kind of a decent grade."

I reply, "Oh, no, you're not! We're going to call the teacher and work through this somehow. You're not going to be penalized because everyone else is being lazy."

Doing Good, Feeling Good

For the past few decades, our society seems to have become less concerned about cultivating self-*control* in kids and more interested in building their self-*esteem*. If we could just make kids feel good about themselves, they would perform better . . . right? At least that has been the theory.

Only recently did Dr. Roy F. Baumeister, professor of psychology at Florida State University, confess that five years of serious research commissioned by the American Psychological Society now show this effort hasn't worked. The *Los Angeles Times* quoted him as follows:

People with high self-esteem think they make better impressions, have stronger friendships and have better romantic lives than other people, but the data don't support their self-flattering views. . . . A generation—and many millions of dollars—later, it turns out we may have been mistaken. . . . I'm sorry to say, my recommendation is this: Forget about self-esteem and concentrate more on self-control and self-discipline.[4]

As the *Times* reporter summarized, "In other words, high self-esteem doesn't make you any better; it only makes you *think* you are better, which, in the end, makes you worse."[5]

Certainly there is value in upholding the worth of every human being. We certainly want our children to know that God made them in His image, and that they are intrinsically valuable to Him as well as to us. We tell them these things often. But in a very real sense, self-esteem is a by-product of self-control. When we live out what we know is true and proper, we feel better about ourselves. When we blow it and fail to live the way that we know we should, those are the times that we feel rotten.

In fact, sometimes the child is more realistic about how he's behaving than well-meaning adults are. If the child is being a brat while the parent keeps up a wishful line of "You're such a good boy," the kid can tell he's being flattered and may decide to act out dramatically. To cite Dr. Morse, the economist and mom, one more time:

Building up a reasonable sense of self-esteem requires a more subtle strategy that disrupts the child's established habits of thought and behavior. Rather than dishing out affirmations, adults can praise the child for specific actions that the child can verify: "You did a really fine job sweeping the steps." The child can see for himself that the steps look cleaner than they did before.[6]

In 2006, another professor, Jean Twenge of San Diego State University, analyzed 16,000 college students regarding narcissism and wrote a book about her findings titled *Generation Me*. The survey she used in her study asked students to agree or disagree with a number of statements, including this one: "I can live my life any way I want to." The vast majority of students agreed. Dr. Twenge found that survey scores had jumped dramatically over a comparable study in 1982.

Reporting on Dr. Twenge's findings, a *U.S. News & World Report* interviewer asked what was wrong with that opinion. The professor and psychologist, who was only 36 years old herself, replied:

> Think about a marriage of two people who both think like that. If I lived my life any way that I wanted to, I would never do any housework, I would never change diapers, and I would never get up with my daughter in the middle of the night.

Later the interviewer said, "You also blame schools for teaching kids self-esteem. Don't you want your daughter to feel good about herself?" Twenge replied:

> My daughter is special to me, but when she's a kindergartner and there are 20 . . . kids in the class, if she was special in that context it would mean that the teacher wasn't paying as much attention to the other 19 kids. I'm not going to tell my daughter that she's special. I am not going to buy her a T-shirt that says, "Little Princess" on it.[7]

The Bible features a list of the fruit of the Spirit, which are the visible manifestations of the Holy Spirit's impact on a person's life. The last one in the list is self-control (see Gal. 5:23). We happen to think the apostle Paul, in drawing up that list, saved the best for last! Self-control is the capstone—it is essential for maintaining peace, patience, kindness, faithfulness, gentleness and the other qualities listed in the passage.

The superlative value of self-control squares with other things Paul wrote. Consider the following:

> Do you not know that in a race all the runners run, but only one gets the prize? Run in such a way as to get the prize. Everyone who competes in the games goes into strict training. They do it to get a crown that will not last; but we do it to get a crown that will last forever. Therefore I do not run like a man running aimlessly; I do not fight like a man beating the air. No, I beat my body and make it my slave so that after I have preached to others, I myself will not be disqualified for the prize (1 Cor. 9:24-27).

> It is God's will that you should be sanctified: that you should avoid sexual immorality; that each of you should learn to control his own body in a way that is holy and honorable, not in passionate lust like the heathen, who do not know God (1 Thess. 4:3-5).

The apostle Peter came up with his own list of eight desirable traits, featuring self-control right in the middle, and concluded by saying, "For if you possess these qualities in increasing measure, they will keep you from being ineffective and unproductive in your knowledge of our Lord Jesus Christ" (2 Pet. 1:8).

Ineffective and unproductive—no parent wants that for his or her child. Building self-control makes it possible for a child to thrive in all areas of life, whether at home, at school, in the community, on the ball field, or anywhere else. It is a quality that must not be ignored or assumed.

Early Steps

It takes work to build this trait into a child. There are no short-cuts. Parents have to be determined from the early years straight through to adolescence that their child will learn and practice self-control.

Bad behavior is a child's way of asking, "Is there anybody who loves me enough to help me gain self-control so that I'll do the right thing? Is anybody big enough to take me on?"

Our answer to that is: "You bet! Here we are. We know what you're asking for, and the world will end before you get away from this vital training." Even when kids sometimes put us to the test, we must not shirk from the contest.

So how do parents instill this all-important quality in their child? They begin long before the first day of public school. In fact, we believe in starting the process so early that you will probably laugh at us.

If you could have watched us right after bringing our babies home from the hospital, you would have heard us talking in a quiet, soothing voice about self-control. The infant would be crying, and we would murmur as we held her, "Okay, now relax—get control of yourself. Mommy and Daddy have this all figured out. It's going to be all right."

Six or nine months later, if you had been hanging around the changing table, you would have heard Kelli say to the wrig-gling baby, "I'm going to change your diaper now. I want you to get yourself under control and lie here for just 15 seconds."

(After the thousands of diapers she has changed, 15 seconds is more than enough!)

Call this brainwashing if you want. But we are entirely serious about building the notion of self-control into a child from the earliest experiences of life.

A two-year-old comes whining for something. Response: "I want to help you—I really do! Now first go in the other room and get control of yourself. Then when you come back to me with a happy face, I'll be happy to help you!"

Preschoolers are notorious for sensing when visitors are around—that's when they come into the room crying for some kind of aid. The whole group then focuses on the child and even sympathizes with him. Again, this is the moment to guide that child toward an empty room, with no "audience" to play to, where he can regain control of himself. Thereafter, you can attend to his need if it is legitimate.

Preschoolers can learn what "stop" and "go" mean. In fact, they had *better* know the meaning of those two words when you approach the street curb or go to the community swimming pool. You don't want to have to rely on physical restraint alone.

Parents of young children talk about the need to "child-proof" their home, by which they mean removing all breakables from reach. Well, what about homeproofing your child instead? Don't you want to get to the place where crystal vases and TV remotes can abide undisturbed in the vicinity of your children? Surely it is good to be able to say to your children, "Don't ever touch the oven door," and have them possess enough self-control to follow through. The same goes for the bowl of candy on the coffee table.

Another example that pops up all through childhood is physical injury. A child falls on the playground and begins shrieking. Too often, the mom freaks out as well. From there, the chaos spreads.

Yes, the skinned knee hurts—we know that. Yes, there's blood. But we don't need to lose self-control. Instead, walk over to the screaming four-year-old and say, "Everything's going to be okay. Get control of yourself. You know, I wonder why God didn't make our blood green instead of red—what do you think? What color would you have chosen?" This distraction serves to calm down the child and return him to rational thought.

Sina, our seven-year-old, recently fell while rollerblading with Dad. He quickly swung back to where she had fallen and said, "Honey, I'm sure it hurts. Okay, do what I do when I get hurt— blow really hard and fast! It'll help the pain go down." He began puffing away (similar to the Lamaze childbirth technique), and Sina imitated him. Within seconds, she was back under control.

We have learned over the years that when a kid tries to talk *through* his gasps of pain, it just heightens the drama. You can't understand half his words anyway because he's crying so hard. Better to say, "I really want to hear you—but please get control of yourself first. Then you can talk, and I'll be able to understand what you're saying."

Naturally, if the child is severely injured, we want to err on the side of grace and compassion. But as soon as we can tell that there are no broken bones and that this is just an upset kid being dramatic, then we insist that they suck it up and return to self-control.

Parties and Playoffs

What happens when a school classmate has a birthday party and doesn't invite your child? Or maybe an older sibling gets an invitation, but the younger one doesn't? Many kids today fly into a spasm of self-pity and complaining. And many a parent tries to fix the situation by saying, "Oh, well, we'll take you to McDonald's instead."

Actually, this is a great occasion to say, "Okay, just a minute. Get control of yourself and tell me what you're thinking." The child will go on to talk about how unfairly she's being treated, how hurt she feels.

You can respond with "You know what? It's really important right now to think about the other kids who do get to go to the party, and feel happy for them. After all, if the shoe were on the other foot—if you were the privileged one who got invited, and Kelsey got left out, you wouldn't like to see her off in a corner pouting about your good fortune, would you? So let's not do that to them. Let's be happy for them."

This is a huge request, we admit. But it shifts the attention outward. It calls on the child to exercise self-control of a different kind—controlling one's emotions.

More than once over the years, we've had moms say to us, "We're having an event at our house, and we were thinking of inviting So-and-so (one of our kids)—but is that going to upset the others in your family?" (They understandably don't feel up to hosting half a dozen Pritchards!)

We respond, "Oh, my goodness, no! You invite whichever one you want—that's fine. The rest of us will be glad about it. Next time, it will be somebody else's turn."

Likewise, in the world of sports, there is huge need for self-control. Sometimes kids (especially boys) get aggressive and do what they know is wrong, such as arguing with a referee or taking a punch at an opponent. Their minds have been properly instructed, but in the heat of the moment, they just don't have the ability to keep their emotions in check.

And of course, when they watch the pros on TV engage in bench-clearing brawls, they aren't exactly getting good examples from athletes they look up to.

Self-control, however, brings multiple rewards. For one thing, it means getting to play instead of being thrown out of the game. And more than that, the young person can take pride in keeping his cool. *That umpire really blew it,* he says to himself, *but I was still able to walk away and keep my mouth shut. I feel good about myself for that.*

In this moment, self-esteem is a by-product of self-control. You can't self-esteem a kid into good behavior. You have to good behavior the kid into self-esteem.

Our boys have tended to be pitchers and quarterbacks. More than once, a coach has come up to David and said with amazement, "Your kid just keeps on pitching, in spite of how the game goes against him. His outfielder drops a pop fly; his shortstop boots an easy ground ball—and he doesn't cop an attitude. He just puts his head down and keeps throwing strikes. How did you get him to do that?"

I (David) say, "Do you really want to know? It's not an easy, three-point answer. This actually started a long time ago, back before he was even walking   "

That same self-control is valuable in the classroom. We want to raise kids who will tell themselves, *The teacher was really unfair to me this time—but I'm going to just keep working. I need to keep quiet and show her on the next assignment what I can really do.*

At home, self-control is the antidote to the common problem known as sibling rivalry. Believe it or not, kids *can* be trained to be generally decent to their brothers and sisters. Yes, it takes vigilance to establish the clear understanding that "We're *not* going to talk that way to each other here in our family." But the rewards are huge.

If we excuse sibling rivalry under the guise of "Oh, that's just what kids do to each other these days," we should not be surprised when those same kids get into spats and feuds on the school playground or in the school hallway. Young people simply cannot turn this behavior off and on. But if they are consistently taught that provocation does not require lashing back, they will get along much better at both home and school.

A different kind of emotion comes into play when romance blooms. Your son or daughter is madly "in love" with somebody, and the desire to explore new territory is nearly overwhelming. Feelings well up inside, aching for expression. Which brings us back to self-control.

A wise father once said to a friend of ours who was just entering this phase of teenaged life, "Son, I want you to remember something very important: You may not be able to control the outside circumstances—what the girl is wearing, how she talks to you, what everybody says kids are 'supposed' to do these days and so on. But you can always control *you*. There is no excuse for losing control of *yourself,* even though the social environment is pushing you in a certain direction."

Whether the challenge of the moment is to keep your scholastic record, keep your composure or keep your virginity, self-control is the key. It makes all the difference, because it's all that separates achievement from disaster.

No Excuses

When a child is out of control, parents often rationalize:

"He's sick."

"She's tired."

"He's just hungry."

"She's going through a phase."

With eight kids, we have been through a *lot* of phases. We know all about the terrible twos, the onset of puberty and all the rest. But we don't accept these as excuses for misbehavior.

Anybody can claim their child has self-control as long as the environment is perfect and everybody's having a good day. But no one's environment is always ideal. School is not always going to run smoothly. Then what?

At certain moments in the van with our kids, we have said to them, "I'm sorry you're hungry right now. We'll eat as soon as we get home in 30 minutes. But you still need to do the right thing. Being hungry is not an excuse to be mean to each other."

The Sunday sermon may on occasion be a little hard for an 11-year-old to follow. But we don't allow slouching or other body language that shows disinterest. We reinforce the fact that God meets with all His people in church, and before the end of the service there will likely be something that connects with each individual, young or old. So we encourage our kids, "Stay tuned and see what happens.

The kids know that the word "bored" doesn't really get accepted in our house. In fact, it generates new ideas from Dad or Mom on how to cure that "boredom": usually a new task to do around the house or yard. So you're better off not to mention it in the first place.

Out of our eight children, five are girls. If you figure their mother into the mix, we have had as many as four females going through their monthly cycle at the same time! The potential for discord during "the week before" has been huge. We have let the girls know that we acknowledge what they're enduring, but they still have to be nice to each other, as well as to us and their brothers. I (Kelli) have said, "Someday you're going to be living with your own husband and have your own kids. Do you want to turn into a snarling tiger each month? No. So you might as well get started controlling your PMS here and now."

We've actually ended up laughing about it together.

Sometimes the two of us look at all the kids streaming into or out of a school and wonder, *Do we really have an epidemic of ADD and ADHD in this country's young people?* That's a controversial question to raise, we know. *But do we really need all the gallons of Ritalin that are being dispensed?* While there are no doubt a fair number of legitimate cases of ADD and ADHD, we can't help wondering how many kids could have been taught basic self-control back at ages four and five and six—and could be medication-free today.

Some of our own kids (we'll not say which ones!) would no doubt have qualified for one of these diagnoses if they had grown up in a different home environment. The message of self-control, which we repeated often from their infancy to the present, has made a major difference in their lives.

Awhile back, Krista, our second oldest, sent us a heartwarming email from college. She mentioned some of the things we'd done, and she wrote about this very topic:

> I see so many kids here at UH [University of Hawaii] hurting so bad 'cause they can't make themselves do what they have to do, to get where they really want to be. They can tell you who they really want to be, they can tell you what they have to do to get there, but when it comes down to making decisions, something isn't there. I am so thankful for delayed gratification, even in the little things all throughout my life. I am so thankful for self-control. Even though I don't exercise it in every area of my life, I am working on it. I love you guys so much. . . .

Self-control, when combined with wholehearted love for God and submission through obedience, form a sturdy tripod for the young person to thrive in public school—and in life. These are not techniques as much as they are bedrock values that shape and inform the whole range of challenging situations. They are indeed the three most important gifts we can give our children.

Notes

1. Edmund Burke, "A Letter to a Member of the National Assembly," January 19, 1791, quoted in *The Works of Edmund Burke* (London: George Ball, 1909-12), vol. 2, p. 555.

2. Jim Holt, "The Way We Live Now," *New York Times,* August 15, 2004. available at http://query.nytimes.com/gst/fullpage.html?res=9F01E7D91F3CF936A2575BC 0A9629C8B63 (accessed November 2007).

3. Jennifer Roback Morse, *Smart Sex: Finding Life-Long Love in a Hook-Up World* (Dallas, TX: Spence, 2005), p. 9.

4. John Fischer, "The Lowdown on High Self-Esteem," *Los Angeles Times,* January 25, 2005, section B, p. 11.

5. Ibid.

6. Morse, *Smart Sex: Finding Life-Long Love,* p. 209.

7. Elizabeth Weiss Green, "It's All About Me," *U.S. News & World Report,* March 12, 2007, p. 22.

CHAPTER 7

The Magic of Being Nice

If kids ought to be self-controlled when they go to school, what about us parents? Of course we know the answer to this question. Practicing it, however, is sometimes a stretch. Especially when we feel our child has been wronged. Nothing quite stirs up our passion like an injustice or slight against our own flesh and blood. The "mother bear syndrome" kicks in, and we're ready to go to war.

The question is not whether to deal with substantive issues and disagreements. The question, rather, is *how* to deal with them, given the fact that public-school personnel get jumped by parents and other citizens about five times a day, it seems. You can tell just by watching their eyes and reading their body language. The minute you walk into their office, they seem to stiffen. They're bracing themselves for the next attack.

Civility has sunk to such a low ebb in our society, and in many homes, that many parents feel justified in spouting off whenever they enter today's school. After all, they've been yelling at their kids at home—and they feel vaguely guilty about that. Now, here is a chance to yell at somebody else *on behalf of* their child for a change. It is almost a misguided attempt to try to balance the scales and "show love." The outcome, however, is not healthy.

Mark Earley, president of Prison Fellowship, said on a recent broadcast, "Anger has become the new norm for public discourse today. . . . Discussion and debate have been replaced with yelling and demonizing."[1] He referenced a new book on the syndrome by anthropologist Peter Wood with the colorful title of *A Bee in the Mouth: Anger in America Now.*[2]

Earley went on to talk about the day the Pharisees dragged in a woman caught in adultery. Jesus, instead of getting into an argument with them, simply stooped down to write in the sand, and then made a quiet but poignant comment about who was qualified to start stoning her. "The Pharisees had come with an agenda, and their anger, like the anger of so many around us today, was merely a symptom of a deeper problem."[3]

It has been our experience over the years that common courtesy—"please" and "thank you"—go a long way to relax the stressed-out teacher or office secretary. They notice it; they are frankly amazed to hear such words from a constituent. Even when we have a legitimate complaint, we still start out with "Hey, how are you doing today?" as we give a handshake, or maybe a hug. We notice the armor start to fall away. The receptionist behind the desk begins to soften as she responds, "How can I help you?"

Basically, this is just the Golden Rule: "In everything, do to others what you would have them do to you, for this sums up the Law and the Prophets" (Matt. 7:12). In our own workplaces and communities, we all like to be presumed innocent until the evidence proves otherwise. We appreciate being approached respectfully and cordially. The same is true of those who work in public education.

Who Are These People, Anyway?

Many parents think they know the principal, the teacher, the librarian; they're part of that large, intimidating public-school monolith that is a lot more sophisticated and credentialed than the average mom or dad. But wait a minute, how does Jesus view these people? What does He think of them?

He loves them. He sees them as incredibly valuable. These are people for whom He died. He earnestly wants them to become His friends, or to continue the friendship they already have. (Yes, large numbers of sincere and godly people are working in the public schools—one of them may just be the person you're getting ready to blast!)

More important than any scheduling issue or grading decision is the need for school personnel to see a Christlike spirit in us parents. These public-school employees are human beings whose eternal destiny we care about. They've met enough religious combatants—they desperately need to meet ambassadors of Jesus.

Here is a test to apply whenever we're getting ready to launch a tirade at the principal or teacher: *If I go ahead and let loose with what I'm thinking, will I still be able to invite this person to the Christmas musical next month at my church?*

Remember, too, that these individuals are not working in a public school because they hate kids. At some point, they started down this career path because they truly cared about young people and thought they could make a difference in the next generation. Who knows how that desire has been nourished—or battered—over the years?

From the principal to the lunchroom attendant, they are all still trying to make their school a great school. We need to give them credit for this. It would be a good move on our part to thank them for this effort. Far too few people do so.

If we truly believe that God is sovereign and in charge, it reduces the number of "battles" that we have to "win." Rather than fighting for our rights, we must pay attention to doing the right thing in the right spirit. He will take care of the outcome.

Missing Facts

Some of the easier conflicts to solve are those in which one party or the other (or both) simply lacks information. We think we know what's going on, but we don't. Let's be honest enough to admit that we parents often get the truth, but not the *whole* truth. Or we get distorted truth.

One wise third-grade teacher made the following statement every fall during her back-to-school night speech, when parents came to visit the building and see their child's room: "As you can well imagine, I hear all kinds of stories from children this age. Eight- and nine-year-olds are very open to talking about anything on their minds. So I'll make you a deal tonight: I'll believe only half of what your kids tell me about you, and you believe only half of what they tell you about me!" This always got a hearty laugh.

But such wisdom is often not followed. Teachers tell us all the time about giving a student a low grade, only to have the parent show up 48 hours later with both guns blazing. Have they actually asked their child what work was to be completed during the past grading period, and did the child do it? "Well, actually, no . . ." Once the facts are on the table, the picture changes considerably.

Sometimes there are information gaps on both sides.

We'll always remember a kid named Mike who began hanging out at our house back in Centralia. Mike played football on the high-school team that I (David) helped coach. He was struggling with his home situation, and we tried to help him get his bearings. We talked about the advantages of doing well in school so that he could go to college someday. Then one day at the beginning of his junior year, he called from school absolutely distraught. This big kid was actually sobbing. "I can't go to college! The counselor just told me that my core GPA isn't high enough."

"He said you *can't*?"

"That's right."

"Wow, that's quite a blow," I replied. "How about if you and I go see him together? I can do it tomorrow."

That sounded good enough to help Mike calm down. On the following day, I gave Mike a pep talk ahead of time out in the hall. "We're not going to go in there and argue," I said. "We're going to be respectful. We're just seeking information. Don't try to defend your position."

We entered the counselor's office, and after saying hello, I began in a quiet voice. "Well, I've been talking to Mike, and he seems to have heard that he can't make it into college. So I told him we'd come in and at least find out what's happening and what it means."

The counselor immediately backtracked, "No, no, no—I didn't say he *can't*. I just said it would be really difficult." He pulled out a file and showed us that Mike was currently carrying a 1.7 grade point average.

"Okay, that helps us understand," I said. "So could you paint the picture for us and help us see where he's positioned academically? What are his possibilities as we go forward?"

From that moment on, we had a cordial exchange. Mike relaxed, the counselor was helpful and we put together a plan of action. I began setting up appointments to meet each of Mike's teachers in an effort to rescue his semester.

In almost every case, the minute we walked in, you could just see the teacher stiffen for battle. They assumed I was there as one of the football coaches, ready to argue for my player's eligibility.

But again and again, I used the soft, polite approach. "Mike was just wondering how he could do better in your class . . ." Within 60 seconds, the teacher would relax and begin to dialogue.

I'll never forget facing the English teacher, whose class Mike was flunking. In fact, I had him wait out in the hall temporarily.

"Hello, Mrs. _____. How are you doing today?"

"Fine."

"I just wanted to talk with you about Mike and how he's doing in your class."

"Ah, yes—everyone wants to talk about Mike!" she responded with caution.

"My wife and I are trying to help him figure out what he needs to do to succeed in his classes. I know he hasn't been performing very well for you. What would you recommend?"

She began unloading on me about his many shortcomings. "And did you know that I've come in early before school to help him, and he's actually stood me up a bunch of times?! He didn't even have the decency to show up at the hour I said I'd be here."

"Well, have you asked him why he hasn't been coming?" I said.

"No."

"Well, just so you know—he's moved to the opposite side of town, a good five miles away. There's only one car in the family, and his dad goes to work very early. The school bus is no help at that hour. So Mike has been walking. But we're getting on toward winter now, and the days are shorter—which means he's having to start out from home while it's still dark. I know he's a big kid—but would you believe he's actually afraid of the dark? It's true!" I chuckled.

"Oh, my goodness, I had no idea," she apologized. Right away she began outlining a new plan to help Mike get caught up. "If he'll do X, I'm certainly willing to do Y, and I'm sure he can pull up his grade to a passing level."

We called Mike into the room and summarized what had happened. We laid out the new game plan. He said he would really do his best.

By the next semester, his GPA was up to a 3.7. It was incredible. He wound up with a full-ride scholarship to the University of Idaho, where he graduated. He is now married and the father of five children.

It all started by approaching teachers with kindness.

Now of course, not every school problem works out this successfully. You don't always get what you want by being nice. But in the vast number of cases, it certainly helps. And whether it "works" or not, we still need to do the right thing.

Bridging Real Differences

Other situations are more complex and involve more than just missing information. Sometimes the wedge issue is real, and both sides know very clearly what it is. They may agree on the overall goal—to have "a great school"—but differ on the route they should take to get there.

A few years ago, a fair number of parents in our local district were upset about several matters: student behavior, academic rigor, communication between the district and the voters (or lack thereof). Accusations and hearsay were flying around, and before long, assumptions were being made about motives that were not very complimentary. Some of the most vocal people were actually pulling their kids out of the public schools altogether and heading for alternatives.

We decided to try to put together an ad hoc group we named Concerned People for Clover Park (CP4CP). A number of parents and other community members joined in to set a different tone to the dialogue. We committed ourselves as a group to "facts, not attacks." We made friends with the administration and spoke kindly but still directly about what was bothering people. We would say things such as "Here's what's going around the community. Is this accurate? Can you help us understand your side of the story?" Then we would go back and pass along what we learned to our various circles of acquaintances.

CP4CP still operates to this day. We have about 100 members. We show up at school board meetings and make presentations. For example, our current principal is a fan of "small-school" theory, which says that if you divide a large school into units of just 350 or 400 students each, things will go better because it's more manageable, kids don't get lost in the mass, and so forth. While that is no doubt true, we believe that it also has the effect of reducing options so that the number of available electives shrinks, especially for upperclassmen. Kids get to their senior year and can't find much to take. They don't want to just fill up their schedule with another P.E. class or a teacher's-aid position. So CP4CP is bringing this issue to light, saying, "It's a problem for some of our kids—now, what can we do to help? How can this be improved?"

Those are magic words in any situation: *How can we help?* They defuse a lot of tension and create a spirit of cooperation between the parties.

It also pays to keep in touch with the larger perspective. Not *everything* is going badly in this school, or any school. Some programs are actually working quite well, aren't they? It helps to state these out loud from time to time. "To put things in perspective, we're pleased with how the math and science departments are functioning. It's turning out to be quite a good year for them. Now there's just one thing that has come up that we'd like to talk about . . ."

We have our disagreements from time to time, of course. Sometimes change takes longer than any of us would like. But at least they're listening, and we're listening. And the process is good for us all. It makes us more of a *community*, not a bunch of isolated houses.

We think this is a lot more productive than the attitude that says, "I don't have time to mess with these people. I'm just going to move my child to the best possible school I can find."

Those who follow that path can unwittingly end up hurting their own property values if the local school district keeps falling down and gets a bad reputation. All of us homeowners have a vested interest in helping the public school succeed.

At the Student Level

We talk with our kids frequently about how to handle the predicament of knowing that the teacher is looking for a certain viewpoint that doesn't jive with our Christian convictions. They will say, "On the test this Friday, what do I do, Mom? Do I say what he wants me to say, or do I stick up for what I believe and take the hit?" This is hard. More than once, our kids have held to their values and accepted a lower grade as a result.

Yet their demeanor of kindness all through the year has sometimes allowed them to get away with more boldness about their worldview. Teachers have liked them enough to cut them slack. Instead of saying, "You idiot—don't you know that God created the world?" our kids have won points with, "You know, I'd like to share with you guys what our family believes about that . . ." or "Here's another way to look at this evidence . . ."

We have also taught our children to use what we call "the appeal process." When a teacher makes a bad decision (they're human, you know), we do not shrink from acknowledging it. Then we coach the kids on how to go back respectfully and say, "Mrs. Smith, I know you said such-and-such. I understand that. I was just wondering if I could appeal that statement. Would you be willing to take a second look at what you said? If you decide to stick with your ruling, that is okay; I will abide by whatever you say. But I just thought I would ask."

When said in the right tone of voice, this can sometimes bring about a welcome reversal. But not always. Either way, it is a good process for kids to learn. They'll be using it in the future with a boss, a pastor, their spouse, and others.

In some ways, this is just the logical extension of the basic civility and politeness we've discussed in earlier chapters. But again, if good manners like this are not taught in the home, they won't be practiced at school.

We have a rule at our house that if you're not being kind to your sibling, don't even bother asking Mom or Dad for permission to go somewhere or to have a friend over. You can't be pleasant to your friend when you've just finished being ugly to your brother or sister.

Another house rule is that if you want something but don't ask for it in the right tone, you have to wait five minutes before asking again. If you blurt out, "Mom, you need to run me over to Kari's house," you'll get nowhere—and you'll have to cool your heels for five minutes before trying again with "Mom, could you please run me over to Kari's house?" The delay is meant to remind you of the need to practice kindness.

With this as a foundation, our kids can grow into kind, polite sons and daughters who are also kind, polite students and classmates.

Blessed Are the Peacemakers

No one would accuse Jesus of being a wimp, even though He did say, "Blessed are the peacemakers, for they will be called sons of God" (Matt. 5:9). That statement applies to more than just national and international diplomats. It also applies to each one of us who lives, works and raises kids in a community.

A couple of years ago, one of the girls on our daughter Jordan's basketball team—a very talented player, by the way—got involved in a conflict with some of the other girls on the team. Hurtful things were said, and Jordan was caught in the middle of it all.

We got to the state tournament that year. At a game in the big Tacoma Dome, we were playing for fifth place. Into the second half, we were losing. This girl's dad, a big man with a very intimidating voice, began yelling mercilessly at the coaching staff. Not long afterward, he and another dad moved down in order to sit directly behind the bench itself, keeping up their criticism.

Somebody needed to intervene. I (David) walked down to sit near them and said, "Guys, this is the girls' big moment here at state—let 'em enjoy it. Let the coach do his job."

"Well, that's the problem—he *can't* coach!" the dad retorted.

"Oh, really? And that's how we got to the state tournament? A lot of other teams never even made it this far."

"Well, it's not because of his coaching!"

By then an assistant coach came up to ask us all to quiet down. The athletic director came down, too. The dad pointed at me and said, "He started it!"

Both of them knew that wasn't true.

The conversation stopped at that point. We ended up losing the game, which meant taking seventh place statewide instead of fifth. On the way out of the dome, more words were exchanged, and I once again felt less than successful at changing the heart of this man.

Six months later, I happened to run into his pastor. We started talking about athletics. I got up the nerve to say, "Mr. _____ goes to your church, right?"

"Yes."

"Well, I was just wondering, have you ever talked to him about his behavior at games?"

The pastor knew exactly what I meant. He had observed it himself. "No, I haven't," he answered cautiously. Then he added, "Maybe you should talk to him about that."

That wasn't the answer I had been hoping for, given how things had gone at the tournament. But I said I would look for an opportunity.

The next year, our son Tana was on a middle-school team with this girl's younger brother. I realized we were going to have to go through another season in close contact with this father.

So I summoned my courage and called him one day. "Hey, I'd love to have coffee with you sometime," I said. "Our boys are going to be playing together this season, and I want to make sure we clear the air, so there's no problem between the two of us."

We set a time. Then he called back to postpone.

I insisted on our getting together somehow. When we finally sat down, I said, "I just need to ask you something. Have I done anything wrong in your eyes? Or has anyone in my family offended you?"

"No, no, no," he answered. "I didn't want to meet with you because I was so embarrassed. You were right that night back at state. I was listening to the 'wrong voices.'" He paused. "After you called back the other day, I went home and talked to my wife. She said, 'Yeah, Mrs. Pritchard is always so nice to me. Why are you hassling them?'"

"Did my Jordan do anything wrong last season?" I pressed.

"No. This wasn't about her at all. This was just my problem. I knew better. I got caught up in the heat of the moment."

"Well," I said with relief, "we really want to be friends with you guys."

"We do, too!" he replied. "Let's have a great season together."

The next time I saw his pastor, he was all smiles. "Way to go!" he exclaimed. "He told me that you guys talked, and that's terrific."

Whether in the classroom, the gym, the cafeteria or the district boardroom, there is always a place for conciliation and kindness. We will never see eye to eye with every public-school official or every parent on every issue. But we can still be nice about our differences.

The Scripture says, "Let your gentleness be evident to all. The Lord is near" (Phil. 4:5). Why did the apostle Paul add that last sentence? Says one commentary, "This may refer to the nearness of the Lord to the believer, or to the nearness of His coming, or both."[4]

In other words, one interpretation of the verse is, *Be gentle because the Lord, though unseen, is right behind your shoulder during this conversation, listening to every word you say.*

The other take on this verse is, *Be gentle because the Second Coming of Christ could happen at any moment—right during your next sentence.*

Either way, it is a good piece of advice that every parent and every child involved with the public school should take to heart.

Notes

1. Mark Earley, "Anger in Public Discourse," aired April 17, 2007, on *BreakPoint*. For a transcript, see www.breakpoint.org/listingarticle.asp?ID-6387 (accessed September 2007).

2. Peter Wood, *A Bee in the Mouth: Anger in America Now* (NY: Encounter, 2007).

3. Mark Earley, "Anger in Public Discourse."

4. *The New Bible Commentary: Revised* (Grand Rapids, MI: Eerdmans, 1970), p. 1138.

CHAPTER 8

Submitting to Authority

How old were you the first time you realized that not every adult in the world was entirely wise, all-knowing and trustworthy? You had gone through the first few years of life assuming that all the Big People knew what they were talking about and had your best interests at heart. Then one day—probably by the third or fourth grade, if not earlier—you found out otherwise.

This is one of the milestones of growing up. The world suddenly becomes a lot more complicated. Someone you have always viewed as a reliable authority in your life turns out to have clay feet after all. Now what should you do?

Authority, the Bible teaches, is a God-given umbrella in our life. If we are willing to live under it, it shields us. If we choose to step out from beneath it, we lose its protection. This is the clear thrust of Romans 13, which tells us, "There is no authority except that which God has established. The authorities that exist have been established by God. Consequently, he who rebels against the authority is rebelling against what God has instituted, and those who do so will bring judgment on themselves" (vv. 1-2).

We immediately bristle at these words, don't we? *Yes, but . . . !* A thousand disclaimers flood our minds.

Before we launch into our speeches, however, we might remind ourselves that Paul wrote this chapter as a Jew living in the Roman Empire—a not exactly humane government administration. The rule of Caesar was pagan to the core, often violent and scornful of minority opinions. No one knew this better than the recipients of Paul's letter—they lived in Rome, the capital city. How could the apostle make such a claim that God had "established" this brutal regime? Hadn't he already been beaten up several times by the goons of crooked magistrates?

Here in the twenty-first century, we have the privilege of voting for our leaders and throwing out of office the ones we find unworthy. We get to choose the president, the senator, the governor, the mayor, the school board. Christians often feel during a political season that they know "God's choice" for a given post. And sometimes, that candidate does not win. Even so, the truth remains that God is sovereign. This overarches all the particulars of Election Night. He is still in charge.

We have to believe this regarding our local schools. Even when we don't understand what God has allowed, we have to trust Him.

When the Roman governor Pontius Pilate (who was not exactly a saint) got irritated with Jesus for not responding to his rapid-fire interrogation, Jesus replied, "You would have no power over me if it were not given to you from above" (John 19:11). If Pilate qualified as a heaven-ordained government official, how much more do the authorities we encounter from time to time? We simply don't have grounds to bad-mouth them or refuse to take them seriously.

Nobody's Perfect

Of course, our own kids don't exactly live under the authority of perfect parents, do they? All of us know we make mistakes occasionally. Yet we expect our children to trust us as God's designated guardians over their lives. We aren't right 100 percent of the time, but God will take care of our children regardless of our mistakes.

It is curious to read the story of Mary and Joseph forgetting to keep track of their 12-year-old boy as they left Jerusalem after the Passover. They just packed up and hit the road, *assuming* (always a dangerous thing for a parent to do) that Jesus was somewhere else in the caravan. How negligent! By the time they finally found him, the preadolescent boy had been fending for himself at least three days. Imagine it—a sixth-grader on his own in a big city for half a week! We shudder at the thought.

Yet the Bible records that at the end of the saga, "he went down to Nazareth with them and was obedient to them" (Luke 2:51). The Son of God voluntarily placed Himself under the authority of a less-than-competent mom and dad. He knew this was His appointed station in life for the time being, and He would submit to it.

The application to school life is obvious. We have been assigned to live compliantly with less-than-perfect school authorities. We are not subversives or underminers; we have been called to show a Christlike attitude by humbly and willingly submitting to their authority.

Today's parents are sometimes too idealistic about public-school leaders. They expect a perfection that they don't demand of company presidents, elected officials and church leaders. Does the governor make the right decision every time? No. But somehow the school principal is not allowed any missteps. This is inconsistent—and unrealistic.

Our job is to take authority as it comes and respond in a mature way. This is not always comfortable. A few years ago, we found ourselves in a tight spot with Jordan, who got shut out of seventh-grade basketball tryouts because we failed to get her permission slip signed and turned in on time. We were only 24 hours late—but the school authorities said, "Sorry, you missed the deadline. It looks like she won't be playing this year."

Jordan was absolutely devastated; basketball is the joy of her life. We responded by going to the principal and appealing for a little grace. It was an honest mistake, we explained, and not all that major. Plus, it was our fault as adults, not hers. Couldn't she have a shot at making the team?

The answer was firm: No.

We moved up one level to the assistant superintendent at the district office, using the appeal process described in the previous chapter. We laid out the facts, admitted our momentary lapse of follow-through and asked for a reasonable variance. She listened to us and then said, "I see your point—it was an honest mistake on your part. But I'm not going to overrule my staff on this. Their decision stands."

By now, we were all heartbroken. We loved our daughter and would do just about anything to help her play *right now.*

One other option lay before us. We could transfer Jordan to the district's other middle school. As a transfer student, she would still be eligible to play basketball. We already knew the coach over there, who was aware of the situation. She commented that she would love to have Jordan on her team. We wondered, *Should we go this route?*

We thought about it, but in the end we decided this would send a bad message to our daughter. It would say that if the authorities don't do what you want, you keep working the system until you get your way. Somehow that didn't set right with the kind of kid we were trying to raise here.

So Jordan stayed at the first school and did not play that whole year. It took a huge amount of self-control on her part— and ours as well—not to mope and get depressed.

But you may be interested to know that it did not derail her career forever. At the time of this writing, she is now a junior in high school, a starter on her team and averaging 10 points a game. Our submission to an unpopular decision by authority carried no long-term repercussions.

The Choice Is Ours

Submitting to authority is a choice. None of us has to do it. We can buck the powers that be if we want, and pay the consequences. It is a decision we each have to make, over and over.

Adam and Eve had a choice of whether to follow their authority in the Garden of Eden. They decided to opt out. And, as the saying goes, the rest is history. The ramifications of their resistance to what God had said echo down through the centuries to this very day.

More than a few times, we have reminded our kids, "You know, God is bigger than this teacher. What you need to do is just honor the teacher and allow God to show Himself in this situation."

It is all right to disagree with a teacher or coach, and to express that disagreement with the boundaries of courtesy and respect. I (David) found myself in this position repeatedly with a former Clover Park High School principal, whose fundamental beliefs about kids and the best way to run a school were quite different from mine. He didn't seem naturally friendly toward kids; you rarely saw him out in the hall to greet them. Students almost seemed to make him tense.

We also experienced awkward moments on the school's Site Council, of which I was a member. The other parents and I would vocalize our disagreements with his strategies, but he rarely changed his mind or reconsidered a decision. It was hard to respect his position of authority.

Even something as simple as the meeting times became an issue. He wanted the Site Council to meet right after school in the afternoons, because that was convenient for him. We said this wasn't good; it excluded working parents from attending the meetings. Couldn't we schedule these meetings for one night a month? The answer was no.

Another issue had to do with a grant application to fund an experimental program. We talked at length in our meetings about what should be written in the document. Then we found out the application had been turned in to the funding agency before it was ever aired for comment. So the Site Council's comments were meaningless. It was exasperating.

All I could say to the man was, "Please don't put us through another showcase exercise that doesn't affect anything. If you truly want our input, ask for it in a timely manner. We're not interested in being just a rubber stamp for things that are already cast in stone." I wanted to say a lot more, of course! But I bit my tongue.

At home, I have to admit my kids sensed my irritation with this principal, which was not a healthy thing. But we did not berate him. We tried to maintain a respect for his office, even though we disagreed with how he was carrying out his duties.

When he finally left a few years ago for a job at Stanford University, he and I actually had a decent exit meeting. We were able to part as friends. He even looked up our son Tavita when he arrived on campus, to see how he was doing.

The lesson in all this is that although we don't design the school system or make all the personnel selections, God has a plan in place. He intends for us to be respectful and cooperative. The truth is, none of us will ever "graduate" beyond life's authority structure. There will always be bosses, pastors and government officials over us—and this structure is actually a good thing. It is not our job to derail it or work around it.

Adults Behaving Badly

We as adults need to be watchful about our attitude toward authority figures, both in and outside the school world. More than once, various kids in our community have been riding in our van, for example, when they started ragging on the local police. The accusations ("racist," "unfair") and the name-calling would grow ever more virulent if we didn't intervene: "Okay, you guys, we don't dis the police in this vehicle. They're here to help us, not hurt us" (something we need to remember when we get pulled over for speeding!).

These days the hostile and inflammatory talk that goes on about authority at all levels is sometimes breathtaking. No wonder kids are insolent. They do what they see and hear from us.

One year during the Christmas holiday tournament season, a female player at our school went up to Seattle to watch a boys' game and got back to school too late to catch the team bus to her own game. She arranged her own transportation and showed up as warm-ups were already underway.

The coach was not happy about this, of course. His response was not to start her that day. Not until the middle of the second quarter did he signal for her to enter the game.

By that time, her dad up in the bleachers was fit to be tied. He had already sent his son, the girl's brother, down to the bench to whisper in her ear, "Dad says if this guy's not going to start you, don't go in."

Now when the coach motioned for the girl to get up, she sat still, shaking her head. "I'm not supposed to go in," she told him.

The coach, surprised, couldn't stop for a long discussion just then, so he turned away and inserted another player. At halftime, of course, he wanted to know what was going on.

"My dad said I couldn't go in," the girl explained.

"Why not!"

"He just said so."

In response, the coach decided to let the girl keep riding the bench all through the third quarter and well into the fourth. The game was tight. As the tension mounted in the last few minutes, the brother was sent back down to the bench, this time to give the coach a message: "My dad says you can put her in now."

Not on your life. This brazen grab for control meant that the girl stayed on the bench the rest of the game. And at the final buzzer, our team had lost.

Within seconds, the dad was in the coach's face. "Why did you do that?! We lost the game!"

The coach, barely managing to keep his composure, replied, "I don't need to answer that."

The dad began whipping off his jacket. "Well, we can step outside and settle this right now!" he snarled.

The coach stared back at him. "I assume you're kidding, right?" He then wisely walked away before things got totally out of hand.

This kind of behavior is what makes our society increasingly ungovernable. Kids think anybody with a big voice and plenty of nerve can change the landscape into something more to their own liking. It undermines the needed structure that makes a civilized community function.

More than once we've heard parents complain, "The teacher just has it in for my Ryan. The two of them don't get along. My child has been 'pegged.'" If this is said within earshot of the child, the situation becomes a standoff between teacher and student.

A more useful approach is to stop debating the teacher's mindset and start approaching the matter as a challenge to be tackled. Far better to say to your son or daughter, "Hey, let's win this teacher over. How can we get her to change her mind about you? Tell me what's been happening."

"I wasn't doing anything bad," the child may protest, "but she thought I was. I told her the truth, but—"

"How did you express yourself to her? Tell me about your tone of voice."

At this, the kid may admit to having an attitude that was a little abrasive. The facts were correct, but the manner in which they were delivered was hostile.

"Okay, let's talk about what to do better next time." Actually, it may require four or five positive, respectful exchanges before the teacher decides she's not just being "played" by the student, that there really has been a change of heart. After all, teachers are human, not robots, which means they remember past interactions. But with persistence, the negative history can be replaced with a pattern of wholesome dialogue—*if* the adult parent leads the way.

Getting the Full Picture

Authorities, of course, need all the facts in order to make good decisions. If a teacher, coach or principal doesn't know the full story, an erroneous judgment will be the result. That is true even in our own homes.

More than once, one of us parents has started to make a decision, only to have the other spouse say, "Uh, before you finish that sentence, may I talk to you just a minute in the other room?" Not all the cards had been placed on the table yet. The child deserved to have us slow down a minute and gather the rest of the facts.

For example, we have a family practice of limiting our children's sleepovers to Fridays and Saturdays only. If there's school the next day, we don't think it's a good idea for our kids to stay up late having a party with friends.

Jordan ran in one Tuesday to ask, "Mom, can I spend the night with Pam?"

"No, it's a school night," Kelli promptly answered.

Jordan started to get upset, and then caught herself. "Mom, can I tell you something else?"

"Sure! Go ahead."

"Erica's mother is moving her back to South Carolina—and we just found out she's flying out tomorrow! This is our last chance for Erica, Pam and me to be together."

Well, that changed everything in Kelli's mind. An exception to the general rule was more than appropriate in this situation.

The same maneuver is fitting at school. We can say, "Mrs. Wilson, may I ask a question first?" Or "Mrs. Wilson, there's something else about this that you might want to know." We are not being difficult when we do this—we are participating in the process by which an authority makes good decisions that affect our lives.

In so doing, kids learn what they need to know for the day when they grow up and assume positions of authority themselves. The statement is true: You can't lead until you learn how to follow. The experience of accepting authority over the years shows us all what motivates followers, what exasperates them, what pulls them together. All of these lessons help build an effective future leader.

Difficult moments in the lives of students are often God's way of molding them and teaching them discernment. Pressure makes us grow. Of course, we can circumvent these trials if we want, making our children feel better in the short term. But if we trust in God's placement, if we stay "under the umbrella" of the authorities He has put in place, our children will come out stronger and more knowledgeable in the end. They will comprehend what makes good followers—and good leaders.

Even as adults, our children will still live under authority. The eccentric junior-high teacher or the stubborn senior-high principal is not the last problem boss they'll face in life. More are sure to come. So they might as well get used to it now. At all stages and in all environments, God is sovereign.

The Old Testament tells the story of a young boy named Samuel, whose well-meaning parents placed him under the supervision of Eli the priest. Samuel actually lived in the tabernacle of God along with the old gentleman. His entire upbringing had been entrusted to this man. We might say that Eli "homeschooled" him.

The only trouble was, Eli was a terribly inept parent. His two adult sons "were wicked men; they had no regard for the Lord" (1 Sam. 2:12). What they did to the worshipers who brought their offerings to God was atrocious—not to mention the brothers' exploitation of the tabernacle's female staff. And Eli did nothing beyond an occasional scolding, which the sons ignored. All this was no doubt watched with wide and wondering eyes by little Samuel. You might think he didn't stand a chance.

Yet he grew up to be a prophet of God and one of Israel's finest judges. In spite of the terrible role models he had as a child, Samuel led the nation as an adult—and proved himself a godly, effective leader. God's sovereign purpose prevailed, regardless of the ineptitude of Samuel's early guide and authority.

The issue is not whether we trust school officials to always do the right thing. The issue is whether we trust "that in all things God works for the good of those who love him, who have been called according to his purpose" (Rom. 8:28).

CHAPTER 9

Teachable Moments

Somewhere in the middle of his sophomore year, Tavita came home from school one day and volunteered, "You know what, Mom? I get offered drugs all the time during gym. Guys are flashing it out of their pockets all the time, saying, 'Hey, wanna buy some?'"

I (Kelli) steeled myself, trying not to show my panic. In a steady voice I replied, "So, how do you handle that?"

"I just smile and shake my head," Tavita said.

"That's good," I answered. Little more was said, until I had a chance to update David that evening. We talked about the fact that our son seemed to be standing solidly against temptation in this case. But should we add anything further? How much should we say, or not say?

David took the opportunity a bit later to share some perspective with Tavita. "Mom mentioned your conversation the other day about guys offering you drugs in the locker room. I guess the only thing I would add is, be sure not to waver when you say no. If you telegraph any hesitation, you'll be dealing with these offers forever. Stay firm, and soon they'll leave you alone. They'll decide you're not worth their sales time."

To Tavita, this made sense; he nodded his head. In fact, he told us later that Dad's prediction had come true. The sellers didn't even bother making their pitch to him anymore.

This kind of outcome can only come about through calm dialogue. If a parent flips out at the initial news ("Oh, that's horrible! Don't you ever talk to that kid again!"), the child will quickly decide to keep his mouth shut from that point on. The information flow will stop. But if the teachable moment is handled sensitively, your kid will keep returning with sentences that begin, "Mom and Dad, you won't believe what happened today . . ." And even though your heart is racing, quietly reply, "Hmmm, tell me more." The longer you just listen, the more news will pour out.

Fight Analysis

Whenever something bad happens at school, we parents have a choice about how to view it. The incident can lead either to a *reaction* or a *teaching opportunity*.

We can fly into the mindset of *I can't believe how awful the schools have gotten these days! I'm getting my kid out of that disgusting place ASAP!*

Or we can step back, take a deep breath and ask ourselves, *Is there potential for learning here? How might this be used to further character growth and maturity in my child?* Sometimes the old saying is true: That which does not kill us makes us stronger.

Children normally do not have the perspective to see this. They're too caught up in the facts of who said what, who hit whom and so forth. It requires parental wisdom to find the lesson hidden amid the drama.

Not long ago Jordan came home and told us about a hallway fight that had taken place that day. Two girls, both of whom wanted the attention of a certain boy, were mad at each other. One of them stole the other's cell phone. This led the other girl and her sister to corner the thief between classes and start beating her up. They used more than fists—one of the assailants had a hard object in her hand, which was never precisely identified.

What did other kids in the hall do about this? They gathered round in a circle to watch! One boy even captured the moment using his video cell phone.

Eventually, another boy courageously intervened, pushing through the circle to pull off the main aggressor. Just then the bell rang, and the cluster of kids dispersed to their classes.

Word spread quickly through the school, of course, via text messaging or furtive phone calls. (Isn't it amazing how fast news travels between kids these days? If there's a car accident, 40 teenagers will show up at the crash scene before the adults even know what's going on. They're way ahead of any parent or police officer. Any crisis in a teen's life seems to get instantly processed with friends.)

The class period wasn't half over before the younger sister of the hallway "victim," plus a friend of hers, showed up at the aggressor's classroom. They marched right in, heedless of the lesson going on, jumped over some desks, and began hitting and berating the girl who had assaulted the sister earlier.

"Stop it!" the teacher ordered, to no avail. "Leave this room right now and go back to your own class!" The pummeling continued until the two girls felt that "justice" had been meted out. Then they left of their own accord.

The school authorities of course summoned each of the parties for confrontation and discipline. They requested the boy's video of the hallway fight so that they could review the evidence; he wouldn't give it up. In the end, the younger sister and her friend who had invaded the classroom got expelled for the rest of the semester.

As Jordan told us this whole sordid tale, we tried not to react. We stifled our instinct to pontificate or generalize. Instead, we tossed the ball back to our daughter: "So, uh, tell us—what do you think about what happened?"

"It was all so stupid," she replied. "Fighting over a boy, over a cell phone—I mean, come on. They just messed up themselves in the end. Nothing got solved."

"What did you think about the penalties? Did the punishment fit the crime?"

Here Jordan wasn't totally satisfied. She thought the principal had been too tough on the avengers and too lenient on the girl who had picked the fight in the first place. Once again it was time to use the familiar phrase "That's interesting." More dialogue followed.

Eventually we concluded that, in a school principal's mind, classroom aggression probably ranks higher than hallway aggression, especially when a student ignores a staff member's direct order. To disrupt the period between classes is one thing; to disrupt formal instruction is something worse. Plus, what happened in the hall sprang apparently from the heat of the moment—a look, a verbal accusation, or perhaps an insulting name. The intrusion into the classroom, on the other hand, was clearly premeditated.

Although the entire episode was regrettable, it did present an opportunity for discussion and even reflection in our family. Kids carry deep feelings about these kinds of events in their lives. They need to process them. Parents can play a vital role at such moments if they listen carefully and then bring wisdom and objectivity to the conversation. The kid is not interested in our summary opinion ("Well, the problem with that is _____"). But they don't want to be brushed off, either ("Oh, you'll get over it"). They want to be heard, to be understood and to emerge with a more complete, accurate perspective.

This kind of dialogue takes time, which is difficult given our "go, go" culture and our busy lives. Some parents are prone to blow off this kind of thing with "Don't worry about it; it didn't involve you" or "Yeah, well—can't you see I'm watching

TV right now?" But these are the occasions when we need to stop and let our child process the incident completely. It is a teaching moment, when we can shed light on how this fits or doesn't fit our overall family philosophy.

When kids process these things with a parent's sensitive help, it improves their lens for viewing life in the future. Next time they won't be so awestruck. They will bring perspective and solid values to the scene.

These are the opportune moments to counter the negative rules of the street that prevail in youth culture today. Some of those rules are "Never, never snitch," "Stand with your friends no matter what" and "Don't put up with anybody's disrespect."

Joseph Marshall, Jr., a former teacher in San Francisco who started a boys' club and a radio broadcast to neutralize the caustic effects of urban culture, writes in his blunt book *Street Soldier* about something he terms *fearship*:

> When the boys in the "hood" say that they stick together and watch each other's backs and slang and bang and steal and murder for friendship, we maintain that they do it . . . for fearship: that is, out of fear what their so-called friends are going to think of them or do to them if they don't go along. Fearship is peer pressure at its most destructive.[1]

He goes on to tell about an Oakland, California, mother who came home from work one night to find her 14-year-old daughter pointing a shotgun at her. Why? The girl was trying to join the Crips gang and had been told that in order to win membership, she would have to kill her mother. The shocked woman lunged for the weapon and wrested it from the girl. Yet even from juvenile jail, the girl wrote a letter asking for a photo of her mother. Why? So she could show the picture to the gang members, who would then go kill the mother on the girl's be-half. The woman was forced to go into hiding temporarily.

That is *fearship* in the extreme—a lie of the street.

Kids in *all* neighborhoods need help sorting out truth from error in what the culture is telling them. Their peers haven't lived long enough to know. They need patient and insightful adult guides.

"Gonna Whup Ya, Dad!"

A much milder example of modern culture's effect on our kids came about one summer when our family was at Wild Horse Canyon, the Young Life camp facility in Oregon. Keila, then eight years old, was down at the gym. "Hey, Dad, wanna play basketball?" he called across the court.

"Sure!"

"Okay. I'm gonna whup ya!" he said with a grin.

In my mind I thought, *This looks like a teachable moment.* So I proceeded to beat him decisively at basketball.

He wiped the sweat from his face and quickly had a new challenge. "Dad, wanna play Ping-Pong? I'll take you there!"

"Okay," I said. I then beat him at the table.

"Dad, how about pool?" he proposed. "I'll kill you at pool. You ain't got nuthin'."

This was bravado he had already picked up from the trash-talking sports culture. It was his simplified version of *I'm gonna tell you how good I am, and how pathetic you are.*

So I went ahead and beat him again, this time at pool.

By now it was time to go inside for supper. On the long walk back to our living quarters, I said, "Keila, remember what we were reading this morning?" It just so happened that our family passages in Psalms and Proverbs that day had included several lines about humility.

He didn't.

Next I asked him, "What do you think of Krista and basketball? How good is she?"

"Oh, she's really good," he answered. He was very proud of his big sister, a high-school senior at the time.

"Have you ever heard her tell you how good she is?"

"No, not really."

"Who's always talking about how good Krista is?"

"Everybody else."

"Yeah. It's really cool when other people say how good you are, you know. Now let me ask you: Do you remember the word 'humility' from this morning's Bible reading?"

It was coming back to him by then. This was turning into a real Deuteronomy 6:7 event, which urges us to talk with our kids about God's principles "when you walk along the road. . . ." We discussed the concept of humility.

Then I added, "Now think about what just happened in the sports center. Wouldn't it have been better to just play me without telling how good you were, how you were going to 'whup' me and everything? Other people could have commented on your skill."

Today, more than three years later, whenever we read those verses in Proverbs, Keila looks up and says, "Like me, right, Dad?" He still remembers the event. He understands what humility is and why he should practice it.

In the Crosshairs

Sometimes the teachable moment comes in the wake of your child not just saying something out of line but actually doing something wrong, like forgetting to turn in a project on time. Now his grade is going to suffer. "Mom, *pleeeease* call my teacher and get an extension, okay? You can do it!" The most loving response is often to step back and let the process run its natural course. The pain of absorbing the penalty will say volumes to the child about planning ahead and meeting deadlines.

On the other hand, your child can do something *right* and still take heat for it. When Krista was captain of her school basketball team, she walked into the locker room one game day to find the place jumping to vulgar rap lyrics. Pregame music is a big deal for athletes; they want to get pumped up before the game starts. On this particular day, a couple of Krista's teammates had brought in some new CDs. The fact that the rappers were insulting and degrading women didn't even register with them. The girls just liked the beat, the energy.

Krista walked over and turned the music off.

"Hey, what are you doing?!" the others yelled. "Leave it on! We like it!"

"Sorry," said Krista. "Did you hear what they were saying about females? We're not going to play that kind of message in here."

"Oh, come on!" A chorus of grumbling went on for several minutes.

After the game that day, we could tell Krista wasn't quite her normal self. She seemed pensive, preoccupied. On the way home in the van, we asked a few questions and soon learned that she was upset about her teammates' reaction; she half-suspected that they had deliberately chosen these CDs to taunt her values.

"I've worked so hard to build unity on this team," she moaned. "We're from a lot of different backgrounds, and I've tried to get us all to focus on playing ball and being a cohesive group. Did I just mess everything up today?"

This led to an honest conversation about how some issues in life are worth taking a stand for—or against. But in fact, we don't stand alone: The Lord is beside us to strengthen us. We talked about what she might do next to let the girls know she wasn't their enemy or their social critic so that they could keep playing basketball together in harmony.

In cases such as this, the following questions are useful for parents to ask:

"Do you need to follow up with anybody? Is there anything that needs to be said now?"

"Do you want me to help you somehow, or can you handle it alone?"

"If this happens again, would you do anything differently next time?"

What About Cheating?

Perhaps the most rampant ill in schools across the nation today—and not just in public schools—is cheating. An ABC News *Primetime* poll found that more than a third of senior-high students (36 percent) were *willing to admit* to a pollster that they had cheated in school. Nearly a fourth of junior-highers (24 percent) owned up to it as well.[2] Who knows how many more cheaters just didn't want to 'fess up?

There's really no point in scouring the Yellow Pages for a "cheating free" school. On this issue, we parents have no choice but to help our kids process this commonplace practice. In talking through the problem with our own students, we've had some interesting discussions. "Yes, cheating is wrong," they've said to us, "but not everybody is just being lazy." Some kids really are in tough circumstances: Their mom is moving them to a new apartment every three months. They have to babysit their little brothers and sisters. The electricity is getting turned off because the bill hasn't been paid. The stepdad or the mother's boyfriend is hassling them. Some kids are even home-less, living on the couch of a friend.

Then we ask, "So what's the most loving thing to do? Are these 'extenuating circumstances' or not?"

Talk about a moral dilemma!

One of our daughters once came up with a reply that we thought was quite good. She would tell kids asking to "borrow" her homework, "Look, I've worked too hard on this; I'm not just going to hand my stuff over to you. But I do want to help you. So here's what I'll do: If you want to come over to my house tonight, I'll tutor you. We can work through this assignment together." This reply quickly sorted out the slothful from those who sincerely needed help. (Perhaps not coincidentally, that same daughter worked as a tutor during college. She earned a lot of spending money in the university's learning lab as she helped students who were struggling. And they earned their grades the right way.)

Pressured to Grow

In all of these situations, the pressure of public-school life is not necessarily a bad thing. It can cause growth in us all. Both generations—parents and our children—can emerge stronger from the experience of wrestling with the difficulties. Remember that wonderful scene in the movie *Braveheart*, in which the princess is trying to dissuade Braveheart from going into battle? She wants to protect him from danger. She doesn't want him to die.

He looks down at her and gives this classic rebuttal: "Everybody dies. But not everybody lives."

Some of the greatest pressures, and therefore the greatest teachable moments, come on the athletic field. One football season when Tavita was our starting quarterback, we were playing really well and building an impressive record, when, for some odd reason, we hit a skid. We lost three games in a row.

At the end of both the second and third losses, the very last play of the game was Tavita trying desperately to pull out a victory—and throwing an interception.

Talk about embarrassing.

I'll never forget that moment after the third game. Although it's a Clover Park tradition for the entire team to walk over to the bleachers after the final buzzer and shake hands with our fans, Tavita, in the wake of this third consecutive loss, was not moving with the rest of the players. Instead, he squatted down and stared at the ground.

I walked over, gave him a quick hug and said, "Come on—let's go."

"Dad, I can't," he answered. "I can't go face all those people."

I wondered, *How should I answer him? Should I just leave him alone this one time and let him work through his disappointment by himself?*

No. I realized this was an opportunity to teach him something very important. I leaned over and said, "You know, there are going to be better days for you as a football player. You're going to win again—trust me. But in order for you to walk over there to your fans on the good days, you gotta do it now, too. So get yourself together, and let's go."

He did.

The next week, he bounced back and won a key game for us. And the week after that, we faced our perennial rivals from the other side of the district, Lakes High School. They (the more well-heeled school) had beaten us 17 years in a row. We badly yearned to get the best of them somehow.

Tavita was absolutely on fire that day. He threw one touchdown pass, then another. By halftime, we had a strong lead. Alumni were whipping out their cell phones and calling their friends to say, "You gotta get down here! We're actually beating Lakes!"

By the end of the game, Clover Park had won 42-21. Tavita had thrown three touchdowns altogether. The entire town was jazzed.

When the hoopla died down, I was able to say to my son, "Now, doesn't it feel better celebrating when you know you did the right thing two weeks ago? You faced your fans responsibly back then, even when you didn't feel like it. Today you get to enjoy the upside."

"You're right, Dad," he replied.

Now he's taking what he learned at the high-school level and putting it to use as he sports the crimson-and-white of the Stanford Cardinal. Someday he'll face even more challenges in his career. He'll be a husband, a dad. The moments of testing will keep coming, not only for himself but also for another generation. Making the most of what life hands us and sorting out what God considers important are key elements in building an adulthood to be proud of.

And for that, every kid can use a calm parent's guidance as well as listening ear.

Notes

1. Joseph Marshall, Jr., and Lonnie Wheeler, *Street Soldier* (New York: Delacorte, 1996), pp. 196-197.

2. Dalia Sussman, "Academic Integrity? ABCNews *Primetime* Poll: Cheating Among Teens Common, Effective," April 29, 2007. http://abcnews.go.com/sections/primetime/US/cheating_poll_040429.html (accessed October 2007).

CHAPTER 10

Up Close and Personal

Why are so many parents nervous at the thought of walking into a public school? We meet moms and dads all the time who find this notion downright scary.

For some, they feel inferior, uninformed and afraid they will say something dumb. After all, *they* don't have a master's degree or a Ph.D. in education like the professionals. Parents don't know all the educational jargon, from "IEP" (Individualized Education Program, whatever that means) to "formative assessment" to "Iowa Test of Basic Skills" (Huh? I thought we lived in Washington).

Others view this as a foray into enemy territory. They reach for the doorknob, assuming that every person on the other side is a hostile, arrogant, godless saboteur of all things decent and positive in America.

Still other parents are haunted by bad memories from when *they* went to school, way back when. Too many trips to the principal's office, too many cold sweats on test days, too many embarrassing moments in the lunch room—it all comes flooding back in their minds.

And for at least some immigrant parents, they worry about their imperfect English. Will they not understand a simple exchange with a teacher or administrator? Will they say something that will embarrass themselves or their child?

To every mother or father who hesitates about setting foot inside the public school, let us say two very important things:

1. *This is about* your *child.* You know more about this child than any of them. And you are the "majority stockholder" here. You were personally commissioned to "train up [this] child in the way he should go and in keeping with his individual gift or bent" (Prov. 22:6, *AMP*), which you know like no one else. His wiring is totally familiar to you. You have every right to be informed about the formal education of your own flesh-and-blood, and even to steer it.

2. *You are a tax-paying citizen of this community.* Without you, these people wouldn't have a paycheck. You don't need to apologize for engaging the system and seeing what they're doing to earn it.

Think about the sheer number of hours you get with your child compared to the number of classroom hours. If a student spends, say, 6.5 hours in school multiplied by 180 school-days per year, that's 1,170 hours over a year's time. Meanwhile, parents have access to the other 9.5 waking hours of the school day, plus all the weekends, holidays and assorted vacations, including summer—a grand total of 4,670 hours per year.

Do the math: School receives 20 percent of the "time pie," while parents control the other 80 percent. That is certainly a sizable advantage that cannot be overlooked.

On top of that, once your child reaches middle school and high school, he no longer has just one teacher—he has a different instructor for each subject/class period. The influence of any one teacher is therefore greatly reduced. Assuming the average student has 5 different teachers throughout the day, each teacher—even the most problematic or ill suited—controls only 4 percent of your child's waking life.

Most educators realize their limitations, we've found. Over the years, we have seen an attitude shift among teachers. Today it's rare for teachers to tell us, "We're the experts; we're the specialists; we know what to do. Just give us your child and stand aside." Instead, what we're hearing more often is, "We can't do this job without parental help. We need you. Fewer and fewer parents these days are making time for their child's school. Would you? Please?"

If you as a parent have a unique gift or talent, schools are dying to plug you in. Teachers are overtaxed and have too little time and energy to spend on enrichment activities. For example, the minute we offered to do a guest unit on Samoan culture, music and art (based on David's heritage), we were welcomed with open arms. Opportunities such as this are more bountiful than we think.

And here is an interesting phenomenon: The rougher the neighborhood, the more welcome you are as a parent! Schools in tough environments get so few parents willing to show an interest (compared to the upscale suburban schools) that they welcome you with sincere appreciation.

Lots of Options

Admittedly, it has gotten more cumbersome in recent years to enter a public-school building, due to security issues. Schools these days have to worry about assailants, sexual predators, feuding ex-spouses having custody spats over their children—the list goes on. The doors are locked; you can't just walk in like your parents used to do. You have to stop at the front desk, fill out a form, show your ID and get a visitor's pass, even if you've been there 100 times. It's a hassle.

But it's worth it. Once the formalities are over and done with, you find yourself in a world of possibilities.

Classroom visits are fine, especially if preceded by a phone call a day or two before. All you need to say is, "Would you mind if I came and visited your class on Thursday?" This is just common courtesy. The teacher may need to tell you, "You know what? We're doing state tests all day, and you would be totally bored. How about Friday instead?"

But don't think just in terms of sitting in the back of your child's classroom and observing. Here are some of the activities that have worked for us:

- Make components for bulletin boards. Every teacher would love help on this.

- Cut out letters for primary-grade classrooms to use.

- Offer to show up in the mid-afternoon to clean the classroom or organize storage shelves.

- Go to the awards assembly that most schools have several times a year—a perfectly normal occasion for parents to attend. It doesn't matter if your child is being honored or not. You still get to the hear the principal speak, watch the various teachers do presentations, see the student body all in one place. You can learn a lot in 45 minutes just by watching.

- Read to kids, especially those who are struggling in language arts.

- Tutor kids for whom English is a second language.

- Be a mentor to a child. Our middle school is *always* looking for people who will go through a background check, get a little bit of training and then commit to spending time with a student on a regular basis. Any community member willing to do this is an automatic hero to the school administration.

- Volunteer to work in the student store. Kelli has learned a ton at our kids' middle school by selling pencils and candy bars in the middle of the hallway. It's a ringside seat that allows her to take in the whole social scene, as kids hang around to talk about how their day is going.

- Offer to help coach an athletic team. Especially in junior high and high school, the paid coaches are always looking for volunteers to help gather equipment, run errands—you name it.

Some things don't have to be done during the workday; they can happen in the evening if that's more convenient for you. Check out these possibilities:

- Phone parents to set up a class party.

- Grade papers at home.

- Work at the school's fundraising auction.

- Join the PTA (parent-teacher association) and take part in its projects.

- Donate materials.

- Chaperone a dance. This will definitely be an eye-opener! There's a lot of action to manage these days. You get to find out who in the student body has a sense of moral restraint and who doesn't. You will also learn some of the background that has shaped individual students. One time David said to a little freshman girl who was flaunting herself way too much, "What would your dad think if he could see you right now?" Her reply was simply a snort, followed by "My dad doesn't care—he's in prison!"

• Go to a ball game. In our part of the country, it seems like parents attend their kids' sporting events consistently during the elementary years but then slack off for middle school, and even more for high school. The empty stands are embarrassing. When you come to the games and cheer for the team, you really get noticed by the coaches and other school personnel. As that great American philosopher Woody Allen said once, "Ninety percent of success is just showing up!"

• Open your home for a pregame meal. This is a wonderful chance to see the athletes in a completely different light. When they're out of uniform and sprawled around your family room chowing down, you learn names, personalities, who's calling the shots socially, who's getting picked on, how your own kids are fitting into the group, and a dozen other things.

Granted, if you feed a football team of 60 big guys, you can run up quite a grocery bill! Kelli's mother was visiting from Florida one time when the team invaded our house for "brunch" before a noon game. She gasped at the magnitude of scrambling 5-dozen eggs, flipping 200 pancakes and stirring up 8 gallons of orange juice concentrate.

Yes, the carpet got dirty that day. But so what? It was a good use of the house God gave us in the first place. When the head coach said, "I can't believe you guys would do all this," Kelli replied, "You bet. We love to serve you in this way. You put in a lot of time coaching this team, and we're grateful for the privilege of helping you get them ready for competition."

Especially for Dads

It's great to have moms involved at school—but when a dad is willing to jump in and help, it makes an even bigger splash. Lochburn Middle School, where our kids attend, has a program called Guys Really Read. Twice a year, they invite sixth- through eighth-grade boys to come to the library on a Tuesday night. Dads and male teachers show up carrying their favorite book.

For me (David), this is one of the coolest things I do at school. I start out the evening by leading the group in a couple of noisy warm-up games. Then we all sit down in a circle, men interspersed with boys. We go around, and each man says, "Here's the book I've read that I totally like, and here's why." He talks for about five minutes. The boys listen intently.

The school librarian, who has been given a list of all our books in advance, is prepared with copies of each so that each boy goes home with a free book. But not, of course, before filling up on pizza at the evening's end (food is always a big draw for boys this age).

It's a great night for boys to figure out that reading is a "guy thing" after all. The principal, librarian and teachers love to have men from the community help demonstrate the point.

If you, Dad, *really* want to hit a home run at your child's school, sign up to go on a field trip. Teachers will practically fall down and kiss your feet. They love having a big, strong man along to ride herd on their rowdiest boys.

Of course, this means taking a half or full day off work. But we take off work for other things, don't we? And some of us (such as myself) have jobs with flexible schedules that can be adjusted fairly easily.

The more of these I've done, the more I've seen the value of having a dad along. When we go to a play or the symphony, boys find out this isn't just sissy stuff. "Hey, guys, this is great! Check it out!" I say. They learn that real men can appreciate the fine arts.

Plus, I'm needed for practical things, such as lugging heavy lunch boxes or escorting boys to the bathroom. How is a female teacher supposed to manage that by herself?

I'll never forget the day I accompanied a bunch of second-graders to the zoo. Everything was going well until, all of a sudden, the teacher spotted one rambunctious little guy halfway up the fence of the tigers' cage! He looked like he was intent on climbing right over the top.

"David, help!" she screamed, pointing in the boy's direction. I got the fun of dashing over there, stretching out my 6'1' frame and grabbing his britches to pull him back down. It was hilarious.

Field trips have become my personal specialty. I love them—and, selfishly speaking, I can get more "P.R." points this way than from anything else I do in our kids' schools. I've taken part in hundreds of outings over the years. I've met tons of classmates and parents whom I would never have otherwise known, and I wouldn't trade any of my hands-on experiences for the world.

Here to Help

In all of these efforts, parents are seeking to become a *known quantity* at the school, a comrade instead of a stranger. You're taking steps toward being on a first-name basis with the principal, the faculty and the staff. At the same time, you are becoming familiar with your child's world—physically, academically and socially. You're getting a feel for its joys and tensions. You're walking the trails they walk.

We've even found it beneficial to get involved a year or two *ahead* of our kids, just to scout out the landscape. If you have a child in fifth grade, think about stopping by the middle school. You'll be better informed and connected when your child actually starts attending there.

Here is the overarching point: No school is going to turn you away if you come willing to serve. What principal or teacher can resist the person who sincerely asks, "How can I help you?" Any latent hostility just melts in the face of kindness and service.

At the very worst, the initial response may be to test you by giving you a mundane task, the kind of thing you consider "grunt work." That's okay. Do it with a cheerful spirit, and watch the doors open thereafter for more substantial involvement.

Friend or Foe?

All of these efforts smooth the way for the day when you have to go in to talk about a concern. You are no longer a mystery man or mystery woman whom the teacher fears. Instead, you're a welcome face. "Oh, yes, David and Kelli," the teacher responds, "great to see you at the game the other night. What's on your mind?"

We've met teachers over the years who were terribly wounded as a result of skirmishes with pushy parents who didn't care one whit about the overall enterprise of education. The only thing on their mind was "Just change my kid's grade so that he can graduate!" In one case, so much pressure was applied that the principal finally gave in and ordered the teacher to make the adjustment. Naturally, that teacher was wary for a long time after whenever a parent called her, walked into her room or sent an email.

Teachers today are getting worn down. They are being taxed for far more than they ever signed up to do when they entered the profession: more paperwork, more reports on special-needs students, more preparation of their students for the multiple standardized tests that the state requires—even impromptu parenting of messed-up kids. In a sense, teachers are getting pounded from two sides at once. Parents are hitting them up for more and more nonacademic services that will compensate for their own inadequacies or even negligence. Meanwhile, the bureaucracy is dumping more and more busy-work on them. Actual honest-to-goodness teaching is getting squeezed in the middle.

They need some allies. When a parent walks in with a smile, gives them a hug and says, "Hey, how ya doin' today? Thanks for everything you're giving these kids. How may I serve you?" they hardly know how to respond. After they pick themselves up off the floor, they will call you their new best friend. This is especially true at the middle-school and high-school levels, where parental involvement has diminished and compliments are few and far between.

At a high school, probably 95 percent of all phone calls to teachers are negative in nature. Rarely does someone call to say, "I just wanted to thank you for all you do." How would you or I hold up under such conditions?

The Parent-Teacher Conference

The baseline occasion for parents to come to their child's school building is, of course, the parent-teacher conference. This discussion of how the student is performing can be merely perfunctory or highly enlightening, depending on how it is handled.

The first step toward making this time valuable is, of course, simply to show up! On time! You would be amazed at how many parents these days just don't bother to write the conference time into their schedule or arrive 20 minutes late.

We believe in both Mom and Dad going. It says volumes to the teacher. *Wow, this couple really cares about what I'm trying to do for their child.* (It also sends a message to your child about how important their education is to you both.)

We go to these conferences prepared to take notes. When we sit down, the teacher typically pulls out a folder and wants to go over test scores. We listen respectfully, even though some of this is "old news" to us, since we've been tracking our child's output all through the preceding weeks. We ask questions about anything we don't understand.

Then, as expeditiously as possible, we move the conversation in a new direction.

"This may seem a little different, Mrs. Keller, but tell us how our child is doing with *you.*"

"Oh, fine. We have a good relationship."

"No, please get specific with us. Does our son seem respectful of you? Does he listen? Does he obey when you ask him to do something? Please understand, we're not expecting a bad report. But we really want to check up on whether he is honoring you as his teacher. That's important in our family."

When she finishes making a response to this query, we move along to other school authorities. "What about his interaction with others, such as the principal? What about coaches and librarians? How does he treat the substitute teachers when you're away?"

Then we ask about classmates. "Would you say our son gets along with other kids, or not so well? Does he speak kindly to them? Or is he sarcastic? Do you ever see a streak of meanness in him?"

Finally, we turn to the area of leadership. "Would you say our child is a leader in this classroom, or not? What do you see that's good in this regard? What, if anything, is a concern? We've told all our kids that it's not enough to stay out of trouble; we expect them to try to be part of the solution, if they can. How would you say that's working out?"

At a recent discussion regarding Keila, our fifth-grader, the teacher told how she had asked him for a big favor: Would he be willing to sit next to a boy who had serious behavioral issues? This child was distracting—the kind who doesn't listen, is hard to be around and often gets other kids in trouble. She had said, "Keila, I need somebody to be close to him and encourage him to do his work. Could you help me by doing that?"

She reported to us, "He said okay, even though I could tell he was not super-thrilled with the idea. I put the two of them together. And it is having a definite effect. When this kid starts acting out, Keila will just quietly look him in the eye and shake his head. And the boy calms down! He truly loves Keila. He considers him one of his few friends in the class."

We don't need to tell you that we parents were bursting with pride at that moment!

These issues—*character, attitude, response to authority, compassion, leadership*—are the real agenda for a parent-teacher conference. It's always good to discover your child's shortcomings sooner rather than later.

One young teacher, in just her third year (but definitely competent), said to us in wonderment, "I've never had parents ask me those kinds of questions about their child!"

We think they are central. That is because we have great expectations for our children—it's not enough that they "pass" or "get by" or "do okay." We want them to thrive in school and keep moving toward the amazing future God has in store for them.

And a key element in this is for us parents to be up close and personal with the school scene, not watching from a distance. As we have said to our kids often, "We're in the public school as a family. We go in together, we come out together. You're not alone. We're right here beside you."

Today, make whatever changes you need to so that you can say the same to your kids. Remember, they need to know they are always supported and surrounded by your love and your desire to be involved in every aspect of their life.

CHAPTER 11

Everybody Should "Homeschool"

When we said back in chapter 1 that we definitely homeschool our children, we were not trying to be cute or evasive.

God gave these children to *us*. He gave your children to *you*. He will hold each of us accountable for their upbringing. We are their first and ultimate teachers. What goes into their minds and souls is our responsibility.

We taught them as little ones how to tie their shoelaces, how to make their beds and how to wash behind their ears. Now that they're bigger, we dare not stop teaching them vastly more important life skills. We must keep doing this until they move into mature adulthood.

Imagine that you had an extra bedroom in your house and an unmarried relative—say, a sister-in-law—came to live with you and your children. Let's pretend that in exchange for room and board, you agreed with her that she would do the cooking for the household. If, as time went on, you began to notice that your kids were being fed more and more salty snacks, abundant quantities of chocolate for dessert and sugary cereals, you would no doubt intervene. You would not just shrug and say, "Well, she's in charge of the food around here. I guess there's nothing we can do."

No, you would assert the fact that these are *your* offspring she's taking care of, and you want them to be fed in a certain way. If necessary, you would begin to write the weekly shopping list and to review nightly menus. You might even step in once again to do the cooking yourself.

The same holds true for the "mind food" your children receive. You care just as deeply about what goes into their brains as what goes into their stomachs—probably more. The need for "nutritious education" is too vital to leave to happenstance.

We firmly believe that if one of our children is struggling academically, it is not "the school's problem" to fix. It is ours. Toward that end, we have made sure that homework gets done. We have purchased software to help a son or daughter catch up. We have on occasion hired a tutor for a subject in which we lacked competence. The ultimate responsibility belongs to us.

A high-school math teacher in another state told us about trying valiantly to get parental help for a student who was basically loafing. He missed class at least once a week and turned in almost no homework; it was clear that he didn't care. The teacher made repeated phone calls in the evenings and finally, on the third or fourth attempt, got through to the mother.

"Hello, I'm Mrs. McCorkle, your son's algebra teacher," she said. "We're now five weeks into the semester, and I need to let you know what I'm seeing." The teacher went on to detail the lack of effort across the board, finishing with a direct request for intervention.

"Oh, uh, well, I'm not sure what to say," the mother mumbled in a soft voice. "Do you think, like, maybe you could talk to him or something?"

Talk to him?! The teacher could barely control her frustration. *That's why I'm calling you! I've talked until I'm blue in the face, I've given him detentions—and his work ethic is just not improving. It's time for some consequences at home, not just at school.* Of course, that's not what she said or how she said it—but it gives you an idea of how difficult a task teachers often have in dealing with struggling students.

We can tell you that if such a phone call ever came to our house, the response would be swift and intense. In fact, we would be embarrassed to have missed prior signals. More than once we have said to teachers, within earshot of our own kids, "You are an extension of us. We are on the same page with you. Whatever you feel you need to do, go for it. If you run into any concern, call us and we'll be here, pronto."

The bottom line here: We view ourselves as the primary instructors, and the classroom teacher as our deputy. The ultimate outcome rests squarely on our shoulders.

No Buck-Passing

One of the temptations for families who use private Christian schools is to relinquish too much, assuming that the faculty on campus are taking care of everything. We hear such parents openly say, "Oh, we're so glad to have our kids attending there. At that school they pray with the students, they take care of the Bible teaching, they even have the kids memorize Scripture—it's the whole package."

Without minimizing the efforts of devoted Christian school-teachers in any way, let us quickly state that Christian *parents* need to be engaged on these topics, too. We want our kids to hear spiritual truth coming from Dad and Mom. If the professionals do all the talking while parents remain silent and simply write tuition checks, a vital voice is missing.

In fact, the same comment can be made about church life. Dropping kids off at Sunday School or youth group is not enough. A child naturally expects the pastor or the class leader to talk about God—that's their job. *But what do my folks think about all this?*

This is why in our family, we insist on sitting together during the Sunday morning worship service. We want to experience the worship, the praying and the preaching together. That way we can talk about it afterward. "Hey, what did you think about the pastor's point this morning on such-and-such?" or "Did you experience any 'God-sightings' today?" (That's a phrase we picked up from Karen Mains's excellent book *Making Sunday Special*.[1]) "Were there any moments when you felt that God spoke to you, either directly or indirectly?"

Too many churches across our country schedule their middle-school or even high-school groups directly in competition with adult worship, holding their meetings at the very same hour so that parents "don't have to be bothered" with their kids. If we went to such a church, we would resist the status quo. We would preserve family cohesion in the sanctuary, because we want our kids to view us as not only their first teachers but "first worshipers," too.

Systems and institutions, however well meaning, must never be allowed to usurp our parental role. We can't abdicate that responsibility for any reason!

The Big Five

When it comes to academic matters, just what do we mean when we say, "Everybody should homeschool"? What are the areas that need the greatest attention from parents? Here, in our view, are the Big Five.

1. Biblical Worldview

The child needs to comprehend what's really going on in this culture: the battle between good and evil, light and darkness; the unique place of God's people in offering His love to humanity; the fact of absolute truth, not just relativistic guesses; the coming day of accountability to an eternal God. To help instill this perspective, we listen to Charles Colson's short daily radio commentary *BreakPoint* (or read it online) and often talk about it with our kids around the dinner table. We also appreciate and use materials from Focus on the Family as well as Worldview Academy.[2] It is essential to give kids "the big picture" about the world in which they're growing up.

2. Creation

The fact that God made our world is often ignored in school as well as in other scientific environments—museums, for instance. We feel obliged to say to our children, "Wait a minute; something's missing from this picture." We don't simply pronounce God's role in creation as an article of faith; we back it up with factual and scientific data from a newsletter we receive from Creation Research, using age-appropriate language.[3] The Institute for Creation Research has very credible information for parents to use, as well.[4]

3. Sexuality

As mentioned in chapter 3, we've opted out of the public school's puberty unit due to its failure to address the moral dimension of human sexuality. But it is not enough just to avoid the questionable; we have to fill the vacuum with something. We have chosen to use such curricula as Dennis and Barbara Rainey's "Passport2Purity" (from FamilyLife.com) and "Preparing for Adolescence" (from Focus on the Family) during special weekends away that each child spends with Mom or Dad, specifically for the purpose of discussing this all-important issue.

We also want to have our own say on such hot topics as the sanctity of human life, same-sex marriage and genetic manipulation. When these come up in school assignments, we quickly provide sources for our kids to explore. If the topic is abortion, for example, we'll say, "Check out what Care Net has to say!" and then refer them to the website (www.care-net.org).

4. American Heritage

Due to a desire to be politically correct, most public schools teach a very skewed, stripped-down version of what guided the founding of this nation. The role of the church in shaping public thought—whether in the Colonial period among the Pilgrims and their successors, or during the modern civil rights movement in the mid-twentieth century—is too often overlooked. We have used such books as *The American Covenant: The Untold Story* by Marshall Foster[5] and *The Light and the Glory* by Peter Marshall and David Manuel[6] to fill in the blanks. We've also talked with our kids about the First Amendment and what is or is not an "establishment of religion." When you explain the religious persecution the Founding Fathers experienced in Europe before they came to America and why they wrote this provision, kids get a more complete and accurate picture of the kind of nation our ancestors envisioned.

5. Spiritual Life and Devotion

We wrote at length about this in chapter 4, but we can't overemphasize this point: The public school is not even going to try to expose young people to God's Word and prayer on a daily basis—and it shouldn't. That is our job. In fact, it is our high privilege. We dare not neglect it because we're too busy or distracted. Nothing is more essential in any of our lives—whether children or adults—than hearing from God and responding to Him on a regular basis.

When?

With everything else going on in a busy week, when do parents find time for this kind of "homeschooling"? We all have plenty of other things to do, that's true. If we are not intentional about this, the weeks can fly by and the urgent can overwhelm the important. But we need to take our role as our children's primary educators seriously—this "homeschooling" business is a nonnegotiable.

Jewish parents in America have historically taken their children to Hebrew school for a set number of hours each weekend, thereby supplementing the public-school experience with training that would make their kids distinctly Jewish. We admire the intent, even though we have not chosen to be that systematic about it. We have, however, done an occasional short course with our kids. When our church, like many others, promoted *The Purpose-Driven Life* for small-group discussion a few years ago, we did it as a family, taking a short break from our usual Psalms-Proverbs morning devotions. One Christmastime we spent several weeks studying the origins of Christmas carols, exploring the character of the writers and the spiritual meaning of the lyrics.

Much of our instruction has come at the dinner table or while riding in the van together. Kelli often clips news items from the paper to bring for discussion. "Hey, you guys, listen to what happened yesterday in New York City . . . What do you think about that?" Moral dilemmas, whether drawn from current events or from a fictional context, provide fodder for lively discussions about ethics.

Sometimes we watch a TV show or take the kids to a movie that we've specifically chosen for its teaching potential. Our older kids wanted to see *Stomp the Yard*, a PG-13 film about two street-dancing brothers, one of whom gets shot. His brother goes off to college, where the dance competition goes to an even more intense level. Taunting and insulting the other dancers is part of the culture.

I (David) went along to the theater that night. It was the beginning of a great conversation with the kids about the place of hostile talk in today's youth environment. In fact, we kept working through this topic for several days.

Other times, a chance to reinforce our worldview will just pop up at random. We get started talking around the dinner table about the war in the Middle East, for example. What does loyalty to one's country mean if you disagree with the current policy? How do you still honor the soldiers as individuals in spite of what they are being asked to do?

Reflecting on the day's events does not come naturally to a child. But it's a valuable habit to learn. That is why Kelli loves saying to the kids as they come home in the afternoon and are getting a snack, "Tell me something exciting that happened today!" or "What really made you feel good today?" If the child is stumped, she'll even push: "Oh, come on—I'm sure some teacher said something good today. You can come up with *one* thing!"

This is much different from the traditional "How was your day?" We never say that, because a child will just mumble, "Fine," and the dialogue will end. We work hard to ask questions that can't be answered in one syllable. We want to engage our children's minds.

Watch the Little Things

When you're paying close attention to your children, you pick up the subtle things. At one point during morning devotions, we noticed one of our kids in the primary grades getting tense whenever it was her turn to read aloud. She didn't want to mispronounce an unfamiliar word. Kelli and I talked privately about what might lie behind this behavior. We came to realize that we had a very diligent, conscientious child here who was so concerned about doing things "right" that she feared to take risks. Some overachievers are like that: They hold back from volunteering to answer a question in case they might get it wrong.

This kind of child is very low-maintenance and generally doesn't cause a ruckus or make a fuss about things. Yet this problem needs attention. We ended up consulting with our daughter's teacher, saying, "We've noticed something when we read aloud as a family—what are you seeing at school? How should we all help in this regard?" By working together for a season, we got our daughter over this hurdle.

Another matter to keep monitoring is the overall balance in a child's life and schedule. For example, enthusiasm for sports should not be allowed to crowd out exposure to music or drama. While a child may naturally gravitate toward social studies or literature, the value of math and science needs to be upheld as well.

I (Kelli) have told my athletic daughters that I want them to compete hard on the court or playing field—but when they come out of the locker room afterward, I want them looking like girls! They need to be grateful that they are young women. Yes, in middle school they had the "tomboy" image as they climbed and ran and swung a bat. But as they've grown up, we've seen them equally comfortable wearing a dress and carrying a purse.

One time Krista opted to feminize her appearance in a basketball uniform by applying matching glitter! For some reason that didn't square with the rules, so she backed off—but then found an alternative. She painted her fingernails on game day in the Clover Park colors of green and yellow. It was her personal statement: "I can be happy and feminine, even while crashing the boards for a rebound or blocking out a point guard!"

Worth the Time and Work

We parents have the high calling of keeping the overall picture in view, managing the many parts and pieces of our children's education. We choose the context. We also set the tone. Kids need to absorb the idea that learning is great; it's fun. At our house we never speak of school in negative tones—you'll never hear us say, "What a downer, sorry you have to go back to school this fall!" On the contrary, we pray aloud in the mornings for our kids to have a great day, to be a light in the hallways, to be part of the solution rather than part of any problem.

This is because we see ourselves as teachers, too. Education is not primarily about "them" (the school). It belongs to us first and foremost. What a privilege we have to guide the effort.

Yes, it's time-consuming. We don't always get eight hours of sleep around our house! "Homeschooling" our kids requires a lot of research. It means reading books and periodicals we wouldn't otherwise get around to reading. People say to us sometimes, "How in the world do you two ever get any reading time when you've got eight kids around?!" Well, we simply make it happen. We have to.

And our kids notice us reading. It's funny these days how we'll be on the phone with our college kids and they'll say, "Hey, you guys have to read such-and-such a book! It's really good." They want us to encounter what they've encountered so that we can then discuss our various opinions of it.

During Alyse's time at USC, she took a course titled "Women in Anthropology." It wasn't long before she was calling to say, "Mom, this is diametrically opposed to everything you've ever taught me!"

Kelli took a deep breath and gave the stock reply of "Interesting—tell me more . . ." Alyse began sharing with her some of the textbook material.

In a subsequent phone call, she described a guest speaker whose views she had found to be especially extreme. She needed to process what she had been hearing in the classroom. In a sense, Alyse was coming back to her "homeroom teacher" for perspective. She had learned over the years to value what Mom and Dad said. Now she was reaching out, even from a faraway college campus, to tap that resource, to lean into that relationship.

Missionary author Elisabeth Elliot once wisely said in an interview, "There's never been a time when children could be successfully raised without sacrifice and discipline on the part of the parents."[7] Maybe little hamsters and rabbits don't need very much parental attention before they're off to the big world on their own, but boys and girls certainly do. When they are nurtured not just physically but spiritually, mentally and intellectually as well, they grow up armed and ready to face adulthood like strong, confident, able sons and daughters of God.

Notes

1. Karen Mains, *Making Sunday Special* (West Chicago, IL: Mainstay Ministries, 2001).

2. For more information, visit Focus on the Family at www.family.org and the Worldview Academy at www.worldview.org.

3. To find out more, visit Creation Research at www.creationresearch.net.

4. Visit the Institute for Creation Research at http://www.icr.org/ for more information.

5. Marshall E. Foster and Mary E. Swanson, *The American Covenant: The Untold Story* (Thousand Oaks, CA: Mayflower Institute, 1982).

6. Peter Marshall and David Manuel, *The Light and the Glory* (Grand Rapids, MI: Revell, 1980).

7. "Happiness Demands Holiness," *Commonlife*, vol. 4, no. 2, p. 5

CHAPTER 12

Your Very Best Chance

By now a fair number of you are probably saying to yourself, *I appreciate what I'm reading here about helping my child thrive in public school—but how would my spouse and I fit this into our already busy lives? We've both got jobs to maintain, and along with all our other responsibilities, I'm not sure we can keep up.*

Let's talk about that.

As the old saying goes, there are no "do-overs" in parenting. We get only one chance to raise our kindergartner. The next year is our only shot at guiding our first-grader. And so on. Before you know it, 13 of these years have zipped by, and our teenager is asking us whether his high-school graduation gown looks okay. It's over and out, so soon.

What is your very best option for getting to that glorious day in May (or June) without a disaster? What will it take to reach the finish line and be proud of the result, not regretful?

We believe we have an answer to that question—but you may not like it. It isn't politically correct. It may not fit your current lifestyle. Do you really want to know?

Bold Statement

We're going to take the risk of stating it anyway, knowing we may lose some readers. Here it is:

> Kids function best in public school if they are backed up by a stay-at-home parent.

This can be either the mother or the father; it doesn't matter. It could even be an aunt or other relative. Whatever the particulars, it simply means a caring adult being available and on top of what's going on every day, every week, every semester—putting into practice the recommendations you've been reading throughout this book.

We declare this not to put a load of guilt on anybody. And we quickly recognize that some people simply cannot pull this off—single moms, for example (we'll address this later in this chapter). But more of us *can* make it a priority to have one parent at home—certainly far more than the 30 percent or so of households currently doing so. And the rewards are huge.

In the vast majority of modern households, the at-home parent will be the mom, so the rest of this chapter will be written by Kelli, who has now been engaged in this lofty calling for two decades and counting. She did not "settle" for full-time mothering due to lack of other options. With two college degrees (B.S. in elementary education, B.S. in social work, completed coursework for a master's), she is in fact more educated than her husband and could have possibly gone out to pull a larger salary. But Job One for her remains the five girls and three boys she brought into this world.

Here's her take.

Lots to Do—and Loving It All

I honestly believe I am a better person as a result of interacting with my kids and their schooling. I've incorporated every bit of my education into my work as a mother. And I love it. This long-term project is incredibly energizing for me.

I certainly don't sit around. I'm going hard all day. There's plenty to do!

The most obvious examples are of course the things that happen during the school day (we wrote at length about these in chapter 10). I show up for class parties, special assemblies and field trips. Whenever one of our children says, "You know, Mom, parents are allowed to come to this thing," I jump at the chance. It's not that I'm catering to my kids; I'm living life alongside them.

School principals all across the nation bemoan the dearth of available moms to help out. Teachers say it's almost impossible to pull off a field trip these days due to the shortage of helpers. Older teachers, who have watched the societal evolution take place, are especially grieved about this subject. They say, "We can't even get parents on the phone anymore, it seems."

If I'm not at one of the kids' schools, I'm home deliberately planning for the three o'clock hour that afternoon when they come bursting through the door. I want the laundry to be done and put away by then, the evening meal already planned and under control, the snack set out and waiting for them. This sets the tone for the next six hours. This is when the magic begins.

If I were distracted or behind on my household responsibilities, things would only deteriorate from there. But if I'm ready with open ears and a clear mind, good things blossom. The child arrives with an achievement to share, an art project to show, a good story to tell. I want to be the person who says, "That's great! You did an awesome job! I'm so proud of you." If, on the other hand, the child has had an absolutely rotten day, I want to be the first comforter and friend. There is simply no way to put a price tag on these sensitive, critical minutes.

For the rest of the afternoon I become the playtime overseer, the homework moderator, the sports practice chauffeur and the all-around organizer. By the time David gets home several hours later, the kids are in a good frame of mind and we're ready to eat.

That doesn't mean the house is in perfect order. More than once, David has arrived to find an unswept patio and a rowdy dog, a family room filled with a tent made from blankets, home-made play dough on the table, flour sprinkled across the kitchen counter, the remains of a cooking project. Meanwhile, I've been saying to the kids, "We're having a great time, aren't we? But it's never quite as good as when Dad is with us." I deliberately pump the expectation that things will kick into a higher gear in Dad's presence.

If I had a career outside the home, I know I'd struggle to balance the many chores that didn't get done during the day. David, instead of shooting hoops in the driveway with the kids, would have to help me get the basics covered. I would be yearning for the kids' attention at the same time he was.

Instead, I'm able to enjoy them from three o'clock on, so that when David comes through the door, I can be generous. "Go on, have fun with your dad!" I say. "Enjoy!"

When I occasionally hear young at-home mothers say, "I'm bored—I need other adults to talk to," it saddens me. I guess I'm the opposite; I have an intense desire to walk with my kids through the growing-up years. I hear myself saying things like, "I'm so glad I had you! Hurry home from school today, okay? I can't wait to spend time with you!" It's a huge privilege.

Not that I don't enjoy adult conversation. I'm active in a women's group called Bible Study Fellowship, and I have a small home business in health/wellness coaching that includes product sales. Most of this happens by phone and computer while the kids are at school, generating a small income for our household. Once in a while, I have to meet with clients during the evening.

But the big thrill for me is spending time with the kids, whether on the school campus, at home or some other place. That's what fires me up.

A Husband's Support

This is what I dreamed of way back in college. I thought about it with every guy I dated, trying to assess whether he would support the idea of my being a full-time mother. I vividly remember talking openly with David about this long before he ever proposed to me. This was the early 1980s, when the feminist wind was blowing strongly the other direction, sounding ultimatums such as "I deserve a career," "Women have been sold a bad bill of goods! We have to demand our place" and (to husbands) "I need equal time away from the kids; you have to change an equal number of diapers."

I could not get myself to join that bandwagon. Maybe it was the result of having been raised by an at-home mother myself, who left her career in nursing to raise us four kids. Whatever the reason, I viewed raising children as my highest calling.

The culture has sold us women a lie. It has said, "Build your outside career, and you'll be happy while your kids will turn out tremendous. With the money you earn, you can provide all kinds of enrichment for them." But is anyone stopping to ask kids what they really want? If we listen, we will hear their little voices saying, "I just want my mom. I want her to show up at my ball games. I want her to be there when I come home. I don't want to have to go to daycare when I'm already tired from a day at school."

How relieved I was to find David backing me all the way. His support has enabled me to stand strong in promoting the value of full-time mothering. He holds me in high regard because of what I do. I couldn't pull this off without his support.

He openly says to others, "What Kelli does here with our children is the most important thing. Of all the work she could have done up to this point in her life, nothing else would have been as valuable. She is the best 'enrichment experience' I can think of. The more the kids have her, the less they need external things. And I will do whatever I have to do to make ends meet so that this keeps working."

He has also talked fairly bluntly with young men (interns in his youth ministry, for example) when they start seeing dollar signs over the heads of their girlfriends, as in "Okay, if I can get a job making $40,000, and she's worth $40,000, that will mean we'll have $80,000 combined to live on." David tells them this is mercenary, short-sighted and self-serving. They need to step back and see the big picture: The next generation needs parents, not presents.

In fact, if you want to put a price tag on our heads, listen to Salary.com, a website that tallies average salaries by occupation. They surveyed 40,000 at-home mothers to learn how much time they put into childcare, cooking, home management, taxi driving and all the rest. Then they multiplied those hours by a fair wage, with overtime pay factored in—and arrived at $138,095 per year! That's what it would cost to hire some outsider to do everything we do.[1]

Can you believe it?!

What About Single Parents?

Yes, it is true that millions of single moms wish like crazy they could be home at three in the afternoon for their children. I have a good friend named Concepción who is singlehandedly raising 4 great kids, ages 14, 11, 9 and 6. She has to work three jobs to provide for her children—and she's also plugging away on her GED. I don't know how she does it all.

On one of my kids' field trips, I met another single mom who is the product of a traumatic childhood and recently left an abusive marriage. She is now raising two wonderful kids alone while pursuing a full-time career.

What are the possible solutions for parents in this predicament?

One, of course, is the help of family members. Many, many grandparents across this nation are stepping in to fill the gaps caused by their daughter's necessary work schedule. For this they should be thanked.

But not every set of grandparents lives close enough to help. This leads me to ask a provocative question: *What about the family of God—the church?* What ministry of care is more important than supporting our own children who don't have a dad and the salary he brings? The apostle James did not mince words when he wrote, "Religion that God our Father accepts as pure and faultless is this: to look after orphans and widows in their distress" (Jas. 1:27). Any church leader who tries to get off the hook by disqualifying those who are alone due to divorce rather than death is merely quibbling. The "distress" a single mother experiences is the same regardless. And the kids need help! You don't have to approve of what caused the divorce in order to take action on behalf of its littlest victims.

What kind of help can a church give the single mom and her kids? All kinds of possibilities come to mind.

- Take care of her car; make sure she doesn't get ripped off at the garage.

- Help her negotiate major repairs to her house (new roof, a new furnace).

- Provide the same backup support when it's time to trade cars or houses. Help her be a wise consumer.

- Recruit a pair of men to be father figures to the children, especially the sons. Have them take the boys fishing, go to ball games or make something together in a woodshop. (Arranging two men for this kind of involvement is better than one so that no suspicions are raised.)

· Provide transportation when needed.

· Fill in whenever the school calls for a daytime conference.

· Make sure the home environment is as physically safe as possible. Ask the mom if she worries about anything in this area, and then do something to remedy it.

· Poll the church members to find an extra washer or dryer—or whatever else the mom might need—that could be given to her.

· Pick up the kids after school and let them spend the rest of the afternoon at your house, playing and doing homework. (I do this regularly for Concepción's kids so that she can have a more relaxing time with them once she gets off work. She has also asked David to help in some discipline issues with her two older kids.)

· Pray for them on a regular basis.

The starting point is to get out of the mindset that says, "Well, nothing can be done. She's in a tough spot, but she'll just have to muddle through somehow. Hope the kids turn out all right." Too often we in the church have passively adopted our society's value system. We take care of our own and let it go at that. We spend our money on ourselves first. We close our eyes and ears to the desperation of others.

Maybe it is time we admitted that the devaluing of the parent role is not something "those terrible feminists" did to us. We've done it to ourselves. We have not held it up for honor in our own circles. We've got to reverse that, and then put our action where our mouth is.

Earlier, we mentioned the marvelous worth of simply asking teachers, "How can I help you?" We ought to ask that same question of every single mom in our churches. There will be no lack of replies. This is what it means to "carry each other's burdens, and in this way you will fulfill the law of Christ" (Gal. 6:2).

A Price to Pay

I cannot pretend that any of this comes easy. Whether reaching out to care for and support a modern "orphan" or providing love and attention to our own children in a two-parent home, it takes time and energy. We all have to make tough choices.

My commitment to full-time parenting has meant giving up some material things. David and I have owned only one new vehicle in 25 years—otherwise we've bought used cars, and driven them until they dropped. We've kept our wardrobes quite simple. We haven't gone on expensive family vacations. Yes, we've done exciting adventures together, but we've kept them low budget.

I hear young couples these days saying, "We're going to wait to have a baby until we can afford it." If that had been our criterion, we'd never have had any of these kids! You can spend boatloads of money on children—the latest clothes, electronic gadgets, summer camp fees, sports equipment, private lessons. Parents have to distinguish, however, between what is a legitimate *need* and what is a *want*. And our kids are going to learn this discipline only from us (heaven knows the world tells them they must have *everything*)—so if we don't practice it, neither will they.

Over the years, God has blessed us with occasional surprises. Sports team organizers in the community have occasionally wanted one of our kids badly enough to waive the fees. One young military couple here at Fort Lewis was being sent to a different army base 1,700 miles away and decided to leave their second car with us so that our high-school kids would have something to drive back and forth to school. It's still running now, five years later, with 169,000 miles on it. Time and again, we have seen God supply something for us that we couldn't otherwise afford.

Couples who are both employed and trying to raise kids pay their own kind of steep price, when you stop to think about it. Yes, the money is more abundant. But too often, a mom comes home tired from work and knows—especially in this round-the-clock digital world—that the boss can still reach her. The cell phone is always there. The email keeps piling up. She looks into the eyes of her child at six o'clock and can't concentrate. She wants to, but the demands of the day keep her preoccupied.

And if the child starts to act up for any reason, the mom too often hesitates to be a disciplinarian. After all, she's been away for the past 10 hours. She thinks, *Maybe it's not really the kid's fault.* She feels guilty when she hands down a serious consequence to a child who might well be just finding a way to get her attention.

My heart breaks for a woman in this quandary. Her loyalty to her children and her dedication to her job are battling each other. It's a no-win situation. How will she feel at the end of 18 years?

There are only 24 hours in a day. When a job preempts time with kids, with one's husband or with our heavenly Father, the woman is definitely the loser.

It's interesting how frequently, when somebody's child gets sick at school, I get an urgent phone call from the mom at work: "Kelli, can you help me out in a pinch? Please, can you rescue my child?"

I don't resent it. In fact, I smile as I reach for my coat and my car keys, remembering the times when classy career women have said to me in days past, "How can you squander your life with just kids?" Well, somebody needs to be available for children. And whatever it costs us, they're worth it.

In fact, I say to my own daughters now finishing college, "After you get married, if you're going to have children only to put them in daycare for 50 hours a week, please don't." Solid research is now showing that every year a child spends in daycare for at least 10 hours a week raises their score by 1 percent on a standardized assessment of behavior problems. The longer a preschooler goes to daycare, the longer the misbehavior persists, even up to sixth grade.

Says Sharon Landesman Ramey, director of Georgetown University's Center on Health and Education, with a touch of irony, "I have accused the study authors of doing everything they could to make this negative finding go away, but they couldn't do it. They knew this would be disturbing news for parents, but at some point, if that's what you're finding, then you have to report it."[2]

When we talk about this research, my girls agree that daycare is not a healthy option. In fact, the older our kids get, the more grateful they seem for how we have done things.

I like the perspective of one Colorado mother of two who is college-educated, a gifted musician and an amazing organizer. Her opportunities in the workplace would be many. But she has chosen to focus on her mothering. She says to her peers, "You *can* 'have it all' as a woman. Just not all at the same time. Life has its seasons. Right now, my season of life is defined by our daughter and son. I'm giving them my best shot. There will be plenty of time later on for other things."

Each and every couple has to make their own decisions about these matters. I fully acknowledge that I can't convince everyone of the importance of having an at-home parent during the school years. That's why we've called this chapter the "best" option, rather than the only option. I simply want to remind couples that if you get locked into a two-income lifestyle and wind up with children you don't especially like, there is no way to go back and do it over.

Children do not successfully raise themselves. They need us. Their attendance at school does not change this fundamental fact. The more we guide, support and encourage them through the years of education, the more we will rejoice at the mature young adults they become.

Notes

1. Dan Serra, "Survey: Stay-at-Home Moms Worth $138,095," *Colorado Springs Gazette* (May 9, 2007), Business Section, pp. 1-2.

2. Benedict Cary, "Study Links Day Care to School Behavior Problems," originally published by *The New York Times,* reprinted in *The News Tribune* (Tacoma, WA), March 26, 2007.

CHAPTER 13

For Men Only

But wait just a minute. The wholehearted dedication of a stay-at-home mom—as valuable as that is—does not constitute the full picture. The unique role of a dad is also a key component in shaping kids for success in school as well as in life. A father's influence impacts a young person both today and for a lifetime, and is important enough that I (David) want to spend this chapter talking about what it means.

I am well aware that not every home has a dad. We all need to be concerned about this and take steps to relieve this vacuum in our communities (as discussed previously). But for those of us men who *do* have the privilege of ongoing contact with our offspring, we need to recognize that we matter—big time.

A 2002 government report said:

Over the last four decades there has been a dramatic increase in the number of children growing up in homes without fathers. In 1960, fewer than 10 million children did not live with their fathers. Today, the number is nearly 25 million. More than one-third of these children will not see their fathers at all during the course of a year. Studies show that children who grow up without responsible fathers are significantly more likely to experience poverty, perform poorly in school, engage in criminal activity, and abuse drugs and alcohol.[1]

Dr. Wade Horn, assistant secretary of the Administration for Children and Families at the U.S. Department of Health and Human Services, told a congressional subcommittee in 2005, "Children who grow up in healthy married families with responsible and committed fathers are less likely to experience a host of negative outcomes compared to those who do not."[2]

We Won't Do a Perfect Job

Few of us would disagree with these statements. Most men I know, however, are troubled by the thought of messing up their responsibility. They feel unsure of themselves, wondering if their influence on their sons and daughters will be all it should be.

To them I say: Hold your hand straight out in front of you, palm side down. Now make a fist. Then, repeat after me as you open your hand: "*Let it go!*" You don't have to be perfect all the time. You're not going to do this father thing perfectly. You're not going to get it 100-percent right. That's okay! What God asks of you instead is that you simply stay in the game.

I remember a closely contested football game during my son Tavita's senior year of high school. I was his offensive coordinator as well as his position coach. We were in the running for the league championship, but we really needed to win this one.

Tavita took one snap on third down and quickly found the pocket collapsing around him as he pulled back to pass. He didn't get the ball off before he was tackled hard for a loss. I could tell he was a bit shaken up. As he walked toward me on the sideline, I saw him reach up and hold his head.

Now, I know all the moms are going to shudder at this next part of the story. But I immediately said to him, "Don't grab your head!" That is because if the trainer saw Tavita holding his head, the trainer would be required, for liability reasons, to pull Tavita out of the game for a doctor's examination.

However, I was the dad here. This was *my* son. I wanted to have him sit down on the bench so that I could check him out myself. I didn't want someone else taking over that decision. "How are you doing?" I quizzed him. "Does anything hurt? Can you see all right?" I peppered him with some further questions, eventually proving to myself that he was generally okay and didn't need medical attention.

Yes, he was a little woozy and might not be able to play his absolute best, but he was still our quarterback. It was important for his teammates to see that he was still *in the game*. In fact, he went on to lead the team to victory in spite of making a couple of minor mistakes. He did not have a concussion or other head trauma after all.

Those of us who are dads need to *stay in the game*, even after we take a hit and feel a little woozy. This isn't the time to grab your head. Shake it off and get back in the action. Your family needs you. You're the man here, and your wife and kids rightfully look to you for leadership.

The main Bible passage that talks about male leadership repeatedly emphasizes loving our wives (and by extension, our children), "just as Christ loved the church and gave himself up for her" (Eph. 5:25). A lot of the current arguments about this passage would dissipate if we focused on its teaching that to *lead* is to *serve*, to *give*, even to *sacrifice*. It's not about dictatorship; it is about giving everything we have for our families, the way Christ gave it all for His church. He "stayed in the game" all the way to Calvary. He didn't bail out when the vigilantes showed up to arrest Him in the Garden, or at any other point. He was the ultimate provider of salvation for those who would follow Him. He is our model as husbands and fathers.

We won't do it as perfectly as he did, to be sure. But we can make it our goal. Here are three specific ways for us to emulate the example of Christ to our families.

1. Take Ownership of "the Buck"

If you are a conscientious dad, you must say, along with President Harry Truman, "The buck stops here." Across our society, the reality is that moms do the majority of child rearing. They typically interact with the school administration, transport kids to games and shoulder the burdens of problem solving. Is this the best arrangement?

I believe one of the main ways for us dads to fulfill our call to servant leadership, as it's called, is to take hold of school issues. I've already talked in earlier chapters about attending teacher conferences and helping with field trips. Beyond these things, I personally aim to position myself as the "go-to guy" for educational matters. Whatever happens, good or bad or in between, I will be alert and involved. The buck stops with me.

Yes, it is true that Kelli does the daily monitoring of homework, keeping track of successes (smiley faces on papers, positive notes from teachers) as well as shortcomings to address. I review the file for each child regularly so that I can give high-fives when merited. If there is a problem, she and I talk it through and map out a solution.

But here is the key: *I'm the one who normally delivers the news to our child.* I'm the one to say, "Okay, it looks to me like you need a 'study table' each night after supper," or "You're showing signs of tiredness and distraction in class, so we're going to move your bedtime up by half an hour." Even if Kelli thought up the tactic in our private conversation, I present it as my idea. This isn't about my trying to pull off a power trip in the family—I'm just making the point that the buck stops with me, and that I'm fully in the game.

In fact, lest you think that Kelli's role is diminished, let me tell a different kind of story. I began noticing at one point that as our kids got older, the rush to evening school and church activities was pulling them away from household assistance. In the past, we had used a "chore chart," but they were too old for that now. The all-too-frequent refrain as the last bites were chewed now became "Hey, I gotta run!" That left Kelli and me with a kitchen to clean up by ourselves. And if I had an evening appointment, I could become part of the mass exodus myself.

Well, I decided this state of affairs needed some attention from The Buck-stopper. I sat the family down and announced that we'd be having a change from that point forward. Since we all enjoyed eating, we all needed to own the clean-up process, too. Therefore, I declared, "No one leaves the kitchen until Mom leaves the kitchen." Everybody would pitch in to clear the table, put the food away, wipe down the counter, wash the dishes and make lunches for the next day. This was only fair. It has been our practice ever since.

We all live busy lives at our house. You do too, I'm sure. There are only 24 hours in a day, and every important activity has to find a place. It takes the conscious oversight of a dad to help make the pieces fit.

No matter how busy I am with my work, I want Kelli and the kids to know that I am always "on call." All they have to do is say the word, and I'll be there. They are the most important people in the world to me. Remember the red phone that used to show up in the old movies—the one that was kept under lock and key so that only a select few could access it? They knew if they ever dared pick up that phone, they would get dramatic results. I want my wife and kids to feel they have a "red phone" line to me. If they need me for any reason, they don't have to worry about whether or not I'll respond.

In fact, it amazes me that Kelli and the kids pick up that "red phone" so seldom. Just knowing they have ready access to me gives them a degree of security. But if something happens at school—or anywhere else in life—that requires my involvement, they know how to reach me quickly. No runaround, no delay from a secretary. They know where the buck stops.

Dads who have openly declared themselves to be *in the game* lend a dimension of reliability and composure to family life. One hundred percent involvement from a loving dad is one of the foundations for healthy living as kids grow up.

2. Guide Kids to Guard Their Hearts

A wise proverb from the time of Solomon says, "Above all else, guard your heart, for it is the wellspring of life" (Prov. 4:23). Another way to say this is, *guard what you care about* or *guard what you love.* Helping kids protect their hearts is another strategic way for fathers to stay in the game.

Obviously, emotions run high in the life of any teenager. And these days, those emotions are translated into action more than ever before. "Nearly every late adolescent has had sexual intercourse, especially males," writes youth culture professor Chap Clark. "Research has shown that the number of teenagers having sex has increased 63 percent in the last twenty years. Seventy percent of males and 60 percent of females have had sexual intercourse by the age of seventeen, and the numbers are 85 percent and 76 percent, respectively, by age nineteen."[3]

You may have seen statistics showing that births to unwed mothers are down slightly. But don't take comfort in that. Mary Eberstadt, former speechwriter in Washington and now a scholar at Stanford University's Hoover Institution, explains, "The number of babies born to teenagers has declined for several years in a row, dropping by 30 percent between 1992 and 2002 for all teens, and 40 percent for black teens. This is largely due to the increased use of implanted or injectable long-acting female contraceptives, or so say the experts."[4] Meanwhile, we are largely ignoring the increase in sexually transmitted diseases among teenagers and young adults. "Of 18.9 million new STD cases in the United States in 2000, about 9.1 million, or half, were found in people between the ages of fifteen and twenty-four."[5]

Every parent of a teenager in public school, and even elsewhere, worries about these trends. That is why I believe a key assignment for dads and other father figures is to help kids live out the words of Proverbs 4:23. Of course, we can't do this unilaterally. We have to pose a question: "Will you allow me to help you guard your heart? Are you open to have me watch out for what grabs your affection during these years, and then bring it up for a talk with you if I think we should?"

This is a discussion too many dads avoid. Why? Because of fear. *I wouldn't know what to say,* they tell themselves, as they let life roll onward in silence. The sad truth is that if we don't speak, the outside world is happy to fill the void. It is eager to define what is cool and gratifying. But we have to be willing to preempt those voices, getting "in the game" to give it our best shot. Even if we do an awkward job, we will at least convey that we care, and we will highlight the importance of the issue at hand.

Along the way, we may be more vulnerable than we would like. Many parents clam up on sexual or drug issues because they fear having their kids discover their own skeletons from years gone by. But you will be amazed how forgiving your kids will be if you're simply honest and open with them.

Among the principles I've talked about with our kids is this important one: "Let's live in the light, okay?" In other words, I don't want us to keep secrets from each other. I promise them that Kelli and I won't freak out if they keep us in the loop on their relationships. We don't want to be meddling in their business—but we do want to know how to counsel and pray for them. The more we know, the more we can support them in their overall goal of doing what is right.

My teenaged girls (and even some of the other girls who have lived in our home) have gone so far as to have me meet guys who are interested in them. When I sit down and talk with a potential date, I keep the atmosphere relaxed—but we actually spend quite a block of time together. My goal is to make sure he knows the young woman he is taking out is extremely precious to me, is loved by our entire family and is very much connected to us all. I also throw in the heads-up that she and I talk regularly about whatever's important to her. So he quickly learns he won't be able to operate behind my back for very long.

Kids today are getting in trouble when they "live in the dark." The societal notion that teenagers should be independent and their dating relationships anonymous is what sets them up for problems. Many other societies around the world look at North American dating customs and shake their heads in amazement. They think we're out of our minds to let kids make decisions—on their own—when it comes to the whole issue of dating. Maybe they have a point.

Guarding the heart has to do with more than just romance and sex, however. It also relates to other emotions that well up inside the young person. Take anger, for instance. When children are steaming mad about something, they need guidance on how to let the pressure out of the tank without scalding somebody. How does this emotion connect with the truth we all profess? One of the best explanations I've heard for the term "integrity" is getting the various aspects of our lives to line up. Integrity means making sure our lives are *integrated*. The head, the heart and the actions all come into alignment.

Dads make excellent coaches at such moments. They say things like, "I know you're really upset about such-and-such. Now, how does this relate to what we read together the other day in the Bible about patience and endurance? How does this emotion you are experiencing line up with what we know to be true?"

When a kid is swept by feelings of resentment and perceived injustice—"It's not fair!"—we have the opportunity to encourage forgiveness and reinforce our bedrock belief in a sovereign God, who works things out in spite of human betrayal. The tides of emotion can be calmed by mature objectivity and faith.

Protecting your son's or daughter's heart means standing up for truth. Sometimes this can be tenuous, but it's far better than the alternative. It means helping your child navigate through one of the difficult challenges of modern life.

3. Anchor Your Family to a Biblical Perspective

I take responsibility for being the spiritual compass of our family. If anybody's wondering where true north is, I hope they automatically look in my direction. I hope they know from experience that Dad has a grip on what the Bible says about current life situations—that he keeps a "God-ward" view of things.

For example, when kids come home from school with questions about what their science teacher said about evolution, I want to lead the research in the direction of revealed truth. I dare not just stay silent and hope they figure it out for themselves.

When somebody's friend or acquaintance at school turns up pregnant, it is my job to articulate the moral problem with this—and also talk about how we're going to respond in a caring way. They need to hear this from a man's mouth, not just their mother's, who is naturally more attuned to the subject of childbearing. But men have something to do with conception too, you know!

Of course, the youth culture today tells kids that there's nothing wrong with getting pregnant while you're single, as long as you take care of the child somehow. That's what my kids and yours are hearing in the hallways. That is why you can read the "Birth Announcements" column in your local newspaper and see that *half* (sometimes more) of the newborns have un-married parents. Who is going to set the record straight?

Another big issue at the moment is homosexuality. Society says it is simply "an alternative lifestyle." They say people are born that way, and nothing can (or should) be done about it. I hold a different view, based on Scripture, and it is part of my responsibility to lay out the biblical framework on sexual orientation for my kids to understand. I also need to talk about what kind of response to people with different opinions would honor Christ. If I don't, the views of peers, secular teachers and the media will rule the day, and we lose the opportunity to stand against sin but still love the sinner. This applies not only to homosexuality but many other areas in life, too. When our children truly understand the nature of sin, and that we are all sinners, they better understand how to respond when temptations come their way.

Teen culture today has a lot to say about what it means to be a man or a woman, when you've "arrived" and how you behave thereafter. In the midst of those voices, we can cut through the chatter and speak truth. To be the voices our kids listen to, Kelli and I use special events to create "rites of passage" that our teens remember long after. We want to be the ones to define the thresholds of manhood or womanhood.

For example, when our first son was about to turn 13, Kelli and I sat down together and wrote a list of character qualities we felt were important for a young man to have. (There's nothing magical about age 13, but historical tradition has often viewed it as a boundary line between childhood and adulthood.) We narrowed our list down to nine key qualities, including confidence, integrity and honesty, among others. I then got busy pairing these qualities with an event I knew our son would find thrilling: a scary ropes course that was nearby. I chose a matching Bible verse for each station along the course. I then set a date to take him there so that he could climb over obstacles and swing from cables 30 feet in the air.

When Tavita was getting fitted for his harness at the start, the attendant explained how it worked and how he could have confidence that the harness would not let him go flying off into space. He'd be a fool, in fact, to try this course without a harness. I then added the application—that as a young man, he should put his confidence in the Lord. He would be a fool to swing out into the future by himself.

We went through each of the nine stations that day and talked about each of the nine qualities. Later on, one of my adult friends who knew what I had planned ran into Tavita. "So how was the ropes course?" he asked. "What happened?"

Tavita's response was quietly thoughtful: "I became a man."[6]

You and your wife may wish to choose a different milestone: a child turning 16, for example, or graduating from high school—or, in the case of a daughter, her first period. Any of these can be useful in defining a new stage of responsibility and growth.

Personally, I have taken each daughter out to a special dinner after high-school graduation, before she heads off to college. The centerpiece of the evening is my presenting her with a ring. Not an emblem of chastity per se, but a symbol of *all* the values my wife and I have sought to instill in her through the years. "Now you will be away from us," I say. "You're going to need to be more self-governing. But every time you look at this ring, let it remind you of what our family believes and what you have gained from us—even though I won't physically be nearby." The gift has always been received with deep appreciation.

These kinds of special events are, of course, built upon a foundation of ordinary anchor points throughout the years. The kids know, of course, that Dad always makes sure they're in church each week. They see me each morning at 6:30 with my Bible open, ready to talk through Psalms and Proverbs with them. These have been vital in creating a biblical worldview for our family to embrace—and to share with the world.

Again, I am not saying that a mother cannot do these things, that familial and spiritual leadership fall solely to the father. Millions of moms are indeed carrying the torch these days, with or without their husband's support. I am simply saying that it means a great deal to sons and daughters when Dad declares, "This is part of my job. This is who I am. This is what I care about. I'm not perfect, but I am determined! What God thinks is what matters intensely to me, and I hope to you, too. That is why I'm staying in the game."

Notes

1. "Promoting Responsible Fatherhood," HHS fact sheet (Washington, DC: Department of Health and Human Services, 2002).

2. Wade F. Horn, Ph.D., "Statement Before the Subcommittee on the Departments of Labor, Health and Human Services Education and Related Agencies," March 8, 2005. http://www.acf.dhhs.gov/programs/olab/legislative/testimony/2005/fy2006_budget_statement.html (accessed November 2007).

3. Chap Clark, *Hurt: Inside the World of Today's Teenagers* (Grand Rapids, MI: Baker, 2004), p. 130.

4. Mary Eberstadt, *Home-Alone America* (New York: Sentinel [Penguin], 2005), pp. 124-125.

5. Ibid.

6. Other coming-of-age plans such as this are available in an excellent book by Robert Lewis titled *Raising a Modern-Day Knight* (Wheaton, IL: Tyndale, 2007).

CHAPTER 14

The Nearest Mission Field

You will notice that we've saved this subject for next-to-last. We did not hit you right away in this book with an emotional call to public-school evangelism.

We thought it was more important to focus on what's best for your child. We've attempted in previous chapters to hold up the values that every conscientious parent wants to instill in his or her son or daughter, and to show how the public school is a useful laboratory for working those out. We have also honestly admitted where the public school falls short, and we've shown how to fill in those gaps.

Now we come to what is still a valid question: Should Christian students and their parents look for any avenue into the hearts and souls of others whom they meet on campus? Do we have any reasonable role to play in bringing them closer to the Savior? Does the Second Greatest Commandment—to love your neighbor as yourself—apply here? Or is it too dangerous to faith that is still young and green?

Demolishing a Myth

Right away we want to set aside The Myth of the Eight-Year-Old Preacher. Anyone who thinks they should fire up their second-grader to go proclaiming the gospel loud and clear on the playground to all the heathen hopscotchers is seriously out of touch. *The main job for a Christian child or teenager in public school is simply to be a good student, a good citizen and a servant-leader—to model what Christianity actually is.* Each morning with our kids, we pray for this to be true.

Meanwhile, the main job for a Christian parent is to do most of the talking with teachers, administrators, coaches, board members, other parents and even their children's classmates—especially in the earlier years. The public-school experience throws us together with all kinds of people holding all kinds of life philosophies. It is our privilege and calling to speak for Christ in ways that resonate with them.

In other words, we should not think in terms of sending our child off by himself to "the mission field." We go there *together.* This is a family expedition. When we show up each August to enroll our kids for another school year, we are enrolling our *family* into the life of this institution. This is a joint venture.

At our house, we reinforce constantly to our kids that they need to deliver a basic level of performance that earns respect from both teachers and fellow students. If your kid is an out-of-control knucklehead in the classroom, you're going to have trouble saying to the teacher some day, "Hey, let me tell you about this great God who means so much to our family." But if your child shows up on time day after day, sits still in the chair, listens respectfully and turns in homework by the deadline, you will be well positioned to get a hearing at the opportune moment.

This is not to say that your child should *never* open his mouth about his faith. It is certainly appropriate (as well as legal) for him to write stories that include prayer or going to church, for example. He can express his opinion about issues of right and wrong. When a controversial topic arises in classroom discussion, he doesn't need to muzzle himself. But again, the *way* he speaks will make a huge difference. If he tells those who disagree with him that they're all "a bunch of sinners going to hell," he won't get far. The words of the New Testament are fitting here: "Always be prepared to give an answer to everyone who asks you to give the reason for the hope that you have. But do this with gentleness and respect" (1 Pet. 3:15).

On the Adult Level

The same advice is good for us moms and dads in our role as primary spokespersons. The people we meet in the school parking lot, on the bleachers and in the parent-teacher association meeting will draw their conclusions about Jesus from what they see in us. We are ambassadors whether we consider ourselves to be or not.

Some of those who watch us are school personnel. Others are fellow parents. And a third group consists of the students themselves.

We'll never forget Leslie, a wonderful kindergarten teacher our son Keila had. Raised Roman Catholic, she had come to consider herself very spiritual, just not "religious."

Her life had taken a tragic turn when her daughter, Holly, had died suddenly of an aneurysm at age four. Several years later, the pain was still sharp in Leslie's heart. She got to know our family through school, of course, and figured out that Keila's older brother Tana was almost exactly the same age as her daughter would have been. She bonded very closely with Tana from that point on.

I (Kelli) began trying to serve her and love her in various ways. Every year on the anniversary of Holly's death, I would pray for Leslie, knowing that she was taking the day off from school. I also made it a point to ask how she was doing during that time. My heart was drawn to her. She became my genuine friend, not just the teacher of our kids.

To this day, we pray for this woman. While some Christian parents might wonder about her spiritual leanings and her influence on their children, they would do well to take time and hear her story. Her instruction of our children on the academic level was professional, and meanwhile, the wound in her soul needed a loving touch.

And she wasn't the only public-school staffer to whom we were able to show the love of Christ. In fact, the former principal at Clover Park admitted one day after getting to know us, "You know, I grew up as a believer, but I've drifted away. I probably need to get back to church, don't I?" He was very supportive of our Young Life work with students on his campus.

When a certain teacher seems to be hard on one of our kids or exhibits a difficult personality, we work at warming up the relationship. We ask our kids as Christmas approaches, "What do you think your teacher would like as a gift from our family? Candy? A book of some kind? What ideas do you have that would let her know we care about her?"

It is a privilege to love school personnel out of genuine interest rather than from a desire to manipulate or push an agenda. They sense the difference. In fact, we love to perplex the nonbelieving educators! They want to pigeonhole us as Bible-thumping zealots, but they can't. As we try to convey the attitude of Christ toward them, the soil of their hearts is tilled.

The same is true of fellow parents. Here the relationship is even more relaxed, because nobody is an "expert." We're all in the same boat raising kids on a stormy sea. More than once, men have come up to me (David) after a football practice or on some other occasion to ask casually, "So, what are you doing to teach your daughters about dating?" Their girls are growing up to become young women, and you can tell the dads haven't given this stage a passing thought. Now they're starting to panic.

This is a question that cannot be answered in five minutes. It takes sitting down together for an in-depth conversation—something I'm quite willing to do. It opens the doors for profitable discussion about life, morals and the future.

Mothers, on the other hand, *have* given the growing-up process a lot of thought—and worry. Small things can become the source of great stress. Two strong-willed moms once got embroiled in a squabble between their two junior-high daughters, who were both friends of our Danielle. It was something about a birthday party that one girl didn't invite the other to attend.

As the moms' blood pressure kept rising, I (Kelli) said, "Time out, everybody. Instead of talking about what So-and-so should have done or not done and who needs to apologize to whom, let's just each of us deal directly with our own daughter on all this drama. Let's get our own girls to calm down. Then let's see if we can guide them toward a reasonable solution. This will show our girls the right way to handle these things in the future."

Both of the women responded, "Oh, I never thought of it like that. Sounds like a good idea."

Sometimes you get the joy of seeing major change for eternity. We will always remember a couple we met back in Centralia. They had two kids in the same school as our oldest two.

He was a contractor and had the rough vocabulary to prove it, even though he said he had grown up in church. His wife as well was far from her religious upbringing. Whenever we were around them, the insults and barbs toward their kids and each other seemed to fly nonstop.

Still, we tried to build a friendship with them. We invited them over to our house, and they accepted. We spent a number of evenings together, trying each time to model courteous behavior.

Their visits to our home became frequent. Then the day came that they followed us to our church. The husband ended up recommitting his life to the Lord. A bit later, so did the wife. We began to notice a change in their tone after that. Kids were treated with kindness instead of sarcasm. God had made a genuine impact on that home.

These are the kind of people you get to influence when you immerse yourself in public-school life.

"Walk-In Business"

The third category of people whom we adults can touch are the troubled classmates of our kids. A football player on my (David's) team—one of the guys who helped eat us out of house and home at the team brunch that Saturday—was without parents. Both of his had passed away. He came up to me at a basketball game one night, gave me a big bear hug and then blurted out, "Hey, whatcha doin' at 5:30 tomorrow night?"

"I don't know—I think I'm free. Why? What's up?"

"Can you guys come to my Senior Presentation?" he wanted to know, looking down toward Kelli. (A Senior Presentation is a graduation requirement in our district, when a student must stand up and do an in-depth speech on a certain topic before a panel of teachers.)

"We'll be there, man!" we shot back. "You bet!" What a privilege it was to show up for a kid who had lost the two most significant adults in his life.

This is what we call the "walk-in business" that God sends our way. We don't drum it up. It just happens as we make ourselves available in the public-school setting, where dozens of kids are on the ragged edge.

Back in the fall of 2001, we had moved to Lakewood and had hardly gotten unpacked when Alyse and Krista came home saying, "Mom, we have *got* to help this girl on our basketball team. She's homeless! Seriously—she's not doing very well in her classes, because her life is such a disaster. She needs a place to stay."

I stared at these two who were already sharing a bedroom as well as each other's clothes. My first reaction was to say, "Girls, we aren't even settled yet ourselves! Don't we have enough kids around here already?" But I held my tongue and listened. We prayed together as a family about what, if anything, we should do. David and I worked through the various angles together. In the end, we invited her to move in with us. She stayed for most of the year.

Emboldened by this experience, we took a little more risk later with a ninth-grader named Bryan, who was a receiver on the junior varsity football team. Our Tavita said one day, "Mom, he's not going to make it through high school unless we help him. Can we?"

"What's his story?" I asked.

"Well, he got busted for carjacking. I think they gave him probation this first time. But if he gets in trouble again, it's going to be bad."

In the back of my mind, I could hear what some people would advise: *You idiot—don't let your son even associate with that kind of kid! What are you, crazy?*

"Okay, let's just start with meeting him first, Tavita. Bring him home after school some day so that we can get acquainted."

Bryan turned out to a likable enough young man. He started hanging out at our house a lot, even some evenings to get help with his classes. Once in a while he would stay overnight. The next morning at 6:30, of course, he had to get up with everybody else for family Bible reading and prayer.

Finally in his junior year, he moved in with us. This was a bit much for Kelli's parents, who said, "What are you doing? This young man has a record!" Yes, but he needed a steady hand to help steer him along. Every Sunday he was sitting beside us in church and listening to biblical teaching. We felt we should continue to stay involved in his life.

There was one funny moment when guests had come to our house for dinner and accidentally locked their keys in their car. What to do? Bryan piped up, "Hey, I'll get 'em out for ya!" And he certainly knew how, in about five seconds flat. We all had a big laugh together.

This is not a pure success story—yet. After graduating from high school, Bryan made some mistakes. But to this day, we still love that boy. He still comes by to see us from time to time, a 19-year-old with a checkered past. He knows he needs to surrender completely to God. We believe God hasn't given up on him, and we haven't either.

On the Student Level

While our young people are called first and foremost to be solid students, opportunities do come along from time to time when they can influence their peers. The older they get, the more often this happens.

But even in the early grades, special moments can pop up. Sina, our youngest, had a new Hispanic classmate in second grade who spoke very little English and really struggled in school. Sina's compassionate heart reached out to her.

One day the girl's mother was summoned to the room for a meeting with the ESL (English as a Second Language) specialist. Apparently, the girl had been hit in the face and was upset. The two adults met back in the corner and tried to work out a solution. But voice levels started to rise, and soon the mom walked out.

Her daughter began crying and ran out the classroom door to be with her mother. When this happened, many of the children in the room started laughing. Sina, on the other hand, saw nothing funny at all. Her eyes welled up with tears at the stress this immigrant family was suffering at that moment. Anyone who noticed her reaction had to realize that this incident cut deeper than perhaps they had thought.

One of our children, while in seventh grade, played basketball on what is called a "travel team," a community-based squad, with a variety of other kids. One white kid, who attended a Christian school, was actually afraid of the African-Americans on the team. Our child, whose skin color is a mixture of Samoan bronze and Indiana white, said to the teammate, "Hey, you're gonna be all right. Don't worry about it. These guys aren't bad. Let's just think about playing ball." It was a privilege to help calm the waters.

The player seemed to relax, although the mother continued to worry. She commented to Kelli that she was relieved about not having her child in the same school with these kids, "having to carry that burden all the time." To us, it was no burden; it was an enriching experience. We love interacting with people, and not just people like us. This has trickled down to our kids.

The campus ministry events these days give students a great opening for sharing their faith with friends. Our kids have always viewed Young Life not just as "Dad's job" but as a tool for them to use. They bring friends to the meetings all the time.

When you see the hope of Christ getting passed from public-school student to student, it's tremendously inspiring. We know a Christian girl, Erin Lutton, who began playing soccer with another girl in sixth grade. She soon learned that the girl's parents were staunch atheists. Life at home, she said, was all about performance and expectations—although there seemed to be an abundant supply of drugs as well.

This young girl and Erin remained friends through junior high and high school, and whenever they went on overnight soccer trips, the girl found it strange that Erin wouldn't join her in smoking pot. But they kept talking. She was curious what Erin thought about life, boys, sex and dating. One day they sat in the car and talked so long they even missed soccer practice.

The other young woman started coming to some Young Life meetings with Erin, although cautiously, because she knew her parents would not approve. Erin and two other Christian friends who played soccer got around that hurdle by starting a Bible study that met early in the mornings before first period. The girl learned much and finally accepted Christ as her Savior just before her senior year.

Her family made life difficult for her—not only her parents but also her two brothers (one in college, the other younger), who had plenty of wisecracks to throw out. She persevered, however. She and Erin volunteered to lead Wyldlife (Young Life's middle-school program) that year. Today she attends Pacific Lutheran University and is still following Christ.

How would this girl have ever been reached had there not been an Erin Lutton on her public-school soccer team?

Hope Extended

As we have said earlier, our inclination in the early days was to homeschool our children. Kelli's personality and training were perfectly suited for the task. She would have been happy, and our kids would have been well served. But something kept chipping away at us on the inside: *What about all those other kids? What if they never hear about the love of Christ?* We could never come to terms with that.

Today, we revel in living out an example of hope to all we meet in the public-school arena. Our kids' friends are amazed to see a married couple who actually love each other and have stayed true to each other for 25 years. So many youth today think that's a complete fantasy that could never happen in real life. We demonstrate otherwise.

We get pulled into the middle of our nonbelieving neighbors—and we're glad about that. If we sat down at our home computer, opened up Microsoft Outlook and analyzed our contacts list of acquaintances from A to Z, probably 40 percent would not be churchgoers. Every one of these names represents a household that is still in need of the light of the gospel.

When Christian parents talk to us about their concerns with public education, they usually bring up three things: (1) physical danger, (2) lack of academic rigor, and (3) intellectual pollution. We counter these concerns by asking gently, "Should we pull all missionary families with school-aged children off the foreign mission field and bring them back to America?" Many of them live in cultures that are antagonistic, even violent, toward the cause of Christ. Many of their children now go to what are called international schools, which teach a wide range of worldviews. They all are immersed in a population that does not uphold Christian values. Yes, they and their kids are at risk.

Yet in the church we honor them as heroes.

What a great opportunity we have in this country to live for God with our children in the middle of "a crooked and depraved generation, in which you shine like stars in the universe" (Phil. 2:15), just like missionary families do. God is bigger than our culture, more powerful than the forces of darkness at work in our world. He has put us here, in this place, at this time, for a reason.

CHAPTER 15

The Moon Is Round

At a conference a few years ago, we heard a wonderful folk singer named Allen Levi. He intrigued us with a song he had written that was inspired by the world of nature. With soft acoustic guitar chords, he began:

> *It is full, then it's quarter, it's fingernail, then gone*
> *At times the clouds will hide it from my sight*
> *The only thing that changes is my partial point of view*
> *But I know the moon is up there every night*
> *When the light cannot be seen, when the circle can't be found*
> *The moon is round, the moon is round, the moon is round.*[1]

His point was that whether you can see God in His fullness or not, it doesn't change His reality. He is still who He has always been—the great and sovereign One. Many times our "partial point of view" keeps us from seeing His awesome power. But that's our problem, not His.

God is in charge, no matter what the public school says or does or allows. God is in charge, whether we and our kids sense it or not. Nothing that happens in any classroom, hallway, office or playing field escapes His attention. His view is better than the most elaborate surveillance cameras. He knows it all.

And He does more than just monitor the activity. We can be "confident of this, that he who began a good work in you will carry it on to completion until the day of Christ

Jesus" (Phil. 1:6). When we don't understand, when we see only dimly or not at all, He still has us in the palm of His hand. We can rest assured of that. At the end of the day, it is not our wisdom as parents, or our maneuvers, or our lobbying efforts or our connections to the powers that be that will make public education a viable option for our family. It is the strength of the Lord.

We human beings have become fairly egotistical, thinking that *we* can control outcomes. Certainly when it comes to the education of our children, we are prone to assume that power and money will rule the day. Professional educators and politicians think the same. But God will have His way regardless. As the wise saying puts it, "There is a God—and you're not Him."

Allen Levi's song says in its final stanza:

> *So I'll write it down on paper, I just might carve it in a stone*
> *To help me when my faith is losing hold*
> *Something to remind me of the Truth that does not change*
> *When the eclipse of the moment steals my gold*
> *There's a Light that is sweet and pure*
> *There's a Love that is strong and sure*
> *The moon is round, the moon is round, the moon is round.*[2]

It is vital for every parent with a child in public school to root him- or herself in the fact that God is full-orbed like the moon, glowing in the dark sky, sure and eternal, despite what he or she sees. Regardless of the clouds churning across the sky, "He sits enthroned above the circle of the earth, and its people are like grasshoppers. . . . He brings princes to naught and reduces the rulers of this world to nothing" (Isa. 40:22-23). The most obstinate principal, the most godless teacher is still under the authority of the Sovereign One.

He's Already There Ahead of Us

We do not have to "take God into the public schools." He's already there! Christians sometimes say the education system today is "such a dark place," as if the God of Light were absent from it. No, He is everywhere. The Ten Commandments may not be posted on the wall, but that doesn't mean God has been locked out of the building. The truth is, nobody loves those scruffy kids in the hallway as much as God does. He is intensely interested in bringing them closer to Himself.

Once in a while the clouds part, and we see Him shining through when we least expect it. I (David) was sitting in a Young Life staff meeting around 10 o'clock one morning when my cell phone buzzed. I stepped away to take the call. It was the Clover Park principal.

"Sorry to interrupt you," he said, "but we've got a problem here, and I thought maybe you could help." He told me that one of the football players (I'll call him Joe) had shown up drunk at school that morning. I knew Joe—he was a Samoan boy, 16 years old.

"Naturally, I have to get him off the school premises," the principal continued. "We've tried to call his mom, but there's no answer. So we were about to call his father—but Joe got really agitated about that. He said, 'Please don't call my dad! He'll beat me up!' So where do we go from here? I hate to just take him to Juvenile Detention."

I recognized this situation as a teenager's cry for help. Nobody gets loaded and then shows up at school without expecting to be noticed. "Let me come over and see what I can think of," I told the principal. "I'll be there in 15 minutes."

When I walked into the office that morning, I somehow had a great sense of calm. I didn't know exactly what I would be facing. But I knew I wasn't there under my own power.

God cared about this kid. He wanted this situation to turn out for good.

Joe was sitting in a chair with his head down.

"Hey, what's up?" I asked, as I sat down beside him and put a hand on his shoulder.

"I messed up," he muttered. He was obviously embarrassed.

"So, I understand you don't want to tell your dad?"

"No. He'll just really go off on me."

"Well," I said, pausing a moment, "we need to. We can't leave your folks out of the loop on this kind of thing. But you're not going to get hurt. I'll go with you."

The principal breathed a sigh of relief. Soon we gathered up the head football coach, and the four of us piled into a car to drive to see the dad.

When we arrived and went inside, Joe slumped on the floor against one wall. The father naturally was uneasy. "What's going on?" he said.

His English was not strong, so I began talking to him in Samoan, which was difficult for me—I'm not that adept at the language. I tried to convey that the man's son was going through a difficult time and needed help. I told him that the fact that his son had arrived at school intoxicated that morning was a red flag.

As I spoke, I was surprised at how the Samoan vocabulary came back to me. I sensed that God was helping me in this critical moment.

Every so often, the dad would murmur to his son, *"Sōsō mai; sōsō mai,"* which means "Move over here; move closer." This was not a friendly thing to say, I knew. He wanted Joe to come close enough that he could smack him.

I kept watching the two of them as I spoke. With every command, Joe edged a bit closer, gradually getting within range. I studied the father intensely—and the instant his arm came up, I lunged between the two of them. His fist still made contact with Joe's head, but it was only a glancing blow. The principal and football coach, of course, were wide-eyed.

"*Áua!*" (Don't!) I ordered the father. "Stop right now. You can't do that. If you do, then we can't leave your son here with you while he sobers up. We'll have to take him into Reman Hall [the detention center]."

The man immediately calmed down. "Okay, Mr. Pritchard," he said. "I'm sorry. I won't hurt him, I promise. We'll be all right."

Everybody sat back down again, and we began talking about how the school could provide counseling for Joe so that he could find better ways to deal with his issues. We spent maybe another 45 minutes together working through a plan to help this young man.

As we drove away that day, I could not help feeling that the Lord had been very present in all that had occurred. His love for this student had extended to every detail of the intervention. I felt humbled to have been given a part to play in this drama. But the ultimate stage director had been God Himself.

No Limits

When we and our children operate out of a daily assurance that God is in control, we can face anything that arises. Over the long haul, we can change entire communities.

What is a community? It is simply a group of people located in a particular piece of geography who are trying to make it, trying to survive. Not many of them consciously want to be bad or difficult or offensive. They are just struggling to get from day to day. This is true not only of "rough communities" but also of "quality communities," no matter what the realtors claim.

In this context, we stand out when we believe that God is sovereign—and that He offers us all a better way to live. We're different. We get noticed.

As we and our children step into the life of our public schools with confidence in a mighty God, communities are changed. Didn't Jesus say, "Anyone who has faith in me will do what I have been doing. He will do even greater things than these, because I am going to the Father" (John 14:12)? If the One who opened blind eyes and raised the dead told us we could top those feats, surely the local school community is not beyond reach. The moon is still round.

Our problem is that we all live our lives within certain limitations and according to certain assumptions. We run on autopilot. We think we're powerless. But then every so often, God bumps us out of our routine for His purposes. He messes up our schedule with an opportunity to help a kid in need, a fellow parent who's adrift or an educator who hasn't been encouraged in a long time. We are almost startled to see what God has in mind for us.

If we go with His flow, it energizes us. Life certainly isn't boring this way. Sometimes our days turn out to be very different from what our calendars said they would be. But that's all right.

The same holds true for our children. More than once, our kids have come home in the afternoon saying, "You won't believe what God did today!" A situation jumped up out of nowhere, and the Lord's hand was evident by the time it was all over.

Sometimes it is a subtle thing. They hear a story from a classmate whose home life is disastrous, and it makes our kids grateful for what they have. "Thanks, Mom and Dad!" they volunteer, appreciative of our being reliable parents. In that moment, they're affirming what kind of parents they want to be a decade or two down the road.

God is bigger than the public school. He "did not give us a spirit of timidity, but a spirit of power, of love and of self-discipline" (2 Tim. 1:7). He can enable us and our children to thrive in this environment, because He has never yet met a challenge too great for His divine purpose.

The Choice Is Yours

We do not expect every Christian family to live like the Pritchards, or do what the Pritchards do. But however God has called you, press ahead. Anchor your family in the living Word of God on a regular basis. Even if you remain in a Christian school or homeschool setting, don't be afraid of the public-school scene. If you are, Satan wins twice. He keeps you and your children in a state of uncertainty about God's power in this world. And he prevents those who need God's love from getting close to the very people who could bring it to them.

We end this book where we started: *You can do this*. We have laid out concrete steps for you to follow. But what matters far more than your game plan or strategic maneuvers is the fact that you serve an incredibly mighty God, and He will prevail. Trust Him on this journey. Walk from school year to school year in confidence that He is on your side.

Notes

1. Allen C. Levi, "The Moon Is Round," © 2001, reprinted by permission. See www.allenlevi.com/moonisround/html.

2. Ibid.

The Pritchard Family

Back row, left to right: Alyse, Kelli, Tavita, Krista
Front row, left to right: Jordan, Keila, David
Dani, Tana, Sina

From Our Children

We thought it might be helpful to add the perspectives of our children regarding their public-school experience. So we asked our oldest four to share directly. At first they worried that it would somehow sound "cheesy" (their term!). But in the end, they expressed themselves very openly, with honesty.

You should know that none of the kids had read this book manuscript (except for a few short passages) before writing their comments.

Alyse, 24

I'm definitely thankful I went to public school. It's part of the reason I'm comfortable in many different social settings. After graduation from high school, I felt well prepared to walk into my first college class—and ended up graduating with honors at USC.

I don't want to sound judgmental of homeschoolers or Christian schoolers. I only know that being in the public school regularly provided me with opportunities for God to reveal Himself to me and grow me into a stronger person. It provided me with a daily challenge to be a follower of Christ, to obey God's commandment to love our neighbors. And I got started in this environment while I still had the daily support system and example of my parents, long before college. I could ask questions and vent my frustrations without ever feeling alone or desperate.

I know there were times when I failed miserably at modeling the fruit of the Spirit. But I can look back now and smile at all the "teachable moments" my parents used to grow me into the person I am today. Public school became an opportunity for them to challenge me on things like commitment, responsibility, organization, and even practice in conflict resolution and the appeal process.

I remember a homework assignment in sixth grade American History. We were to write a paragraph on the definition of tolerance. It would have been easy for me to look up the word in the dictionary and then just paraphrase a little section. Luckily, my dad noticed what I was doing and turned it into an insightful lesson. He saw the assignment as an opportunity to talk to me about absolute truth, freedom of religion, and the separation of church and state. We also got into the whole issue of our need to accept all people as God's children without having to accept all people's beliefs and actions as righteous in God's eyes.

In a number of my college courses, professors discussed the topic of diversity in the classroom, especially how the learning experience is enhanced through the collaboration of ideas and beliefs. They used the example of a class debate, and how much more valuable and insightful the discussion becomes when participants represent a broad range of religions, races and cultures. In that context, I was able to appreciate the differences in others without buying into the trap of relative truth. Instead of feeling like a victim or a target during intense debates, I was actually grateful for the challenge.

My faith didn't collapse under the stress of controversy, although there were many occasions I found myself calling my parents right after class to continue a dialogue. During my public-school days, I had formed the habit of seeking advice and counsel beyond my teachers and textbooks, and that didn't change down the road.

Krista, 22

In a public-school setting, I had the opportunity to live out what Jesus prayed about His disciples being in the world but not of the world (see John 17:13-16). I know this is where God wanted me.

I fully understand that public schools are not the only places where this could be accomplished. But I also know that, for me, they helped build my character, challenged my understanding and taught me to stand alone.

In the academic arena of the public schools, my faith was and still is constantly challenged. Secular teaching often goes against what we learn in Sunday School. As a result of these conflicting authorities, many students separate school from faith. My parents, however, told us every day before we left for school, "Remember who you are." That meant, first and foremost, a child of God. My parents have done an amazing job using public-school situations to teach us to filter everything through that identity.

We learned to use them to grow our faith and really seek out discernment about what we believe, instead of being scared that we were hearing the wrong information. I learned to use confusion as a path into the quest for ultimate truth that otherwise I may have never taken.

My parents always say, "Don't let school get in the way of your child's education." They certainly didn't. After all, we were only at school six hours a day. Every night at the dinner table, every morning at 6:30 devotions, and anytime there was anything going on, we talked, and talked and talked. This not only gave my parents the opportunity to teach us life lessons, but they also got to be the mentors in developing our ability to process anything we encountered.

During my years in public school, I have had amazing teachers—and really terrible teachers. I have learned so much from both kinds. Having multiple teachers really helped me understand my learning style. Most importantly, multiple teachers in my career have sparked significant interest in areas of life I had no idea existed.

My experience with school athletics is probably responsible for a great deal of who I am today. Discipline, work ethic, diligence, the need to work with others, and respect for authority are only a few of the major elements of being an athlete and belonging to a team. This is where my parents' next quote comes into play: "Don't worry about the things you can't control." I often had to work hard to do my part when no one else was doing theirs, and to be okay with that. I learned to respect authority, even when I didn't agree with it. That was valuable on the basketball court and in the field; it is even more valuable today.

Public school involves diverse lifestyles, races, ethnicities, social status, belief systems and overall backgrounds. Finding ways to relate to all kinds of different people is very beneficial for growth and maturity. Beyond that, it is part of our calling. As Young Life puts it in its mission statement, we are meant to "earn the right to be heard."

Tavita, 20

I am most definitely glad I went to public schools. It gave me opportunities and experiences I don't think I would have had in a private-school setting.

The Pritchard household is somewhat well known in the Clover Park High School community. This made it very easy for many of my friends—especially football players—to come over early and often. It was a tremendous blessing to have my family and my house to bring them to. They got to observe my home and family and see how I was living my life. They saw and respected that.

Please don't think that I had an ulterior motive in hanging out with these guys—that I was the "good Christian kid" in public school in order to save them. I was just genuinely drawn to these other kids and cared about them.

The best thing my parents did in guiding us through public school was simply to make themselves available. If I had questions or concerns about anything, I could go to my dad at any time and ask. They were also very proactive in their approach to the public school and didn't leave much unexamined. I'm not saying we had an answer for every situation we faced in school. But we had ingrained in us the concept of right and wrong and a pretty good grasp of how to handle potential problem spots.

It is definitely not my intention here to be critical of private schools or home schools. I just know that in my case, the public school was a tremendously positive experience.

Jordan, 17

Public school is the place where I've learned to trust my faith and prove my faith firsthand. I would not have had it any other way. Granted, I might have seen some of the same in private school, but not to the degree I have experienced.

Public school has prepared me for more of the real world, which includes every culture and every social class. And certainly I will encounter an even more diverse mix of people in the future.

School is always exciting, providing a teachable moment every day. I never realized how much my training as a child would reflect in high school. My parents always brought up teachable moments when I was a child, and they continue to do so today. For example, the first thing they ask is not who won the fight but what the right thing would have been to do. It really does make me think, and it sticks in my mind every day.

If you ask me what's the hardest part of public school, I would have to say it's standing out. Sometimes I do feel out of place at school. This was especially true in middle school, when I was the new kid who had just come to this area from Centralia. But now in high school when close friends of mine apologize for their past actions toward me and tell me of their commitments to Christ, I thank God that I stuck it out.

Being different is not easy, especially when you have to do something your friends think is dumb—for example, standing up for the underdog. This is something our family has always been big on. We've always been taught to stand up for those kids who cannot stand up for themselves. And I frequently get ridiculed for doing so. But when that kid thanks me for helping him, or a teacher tells me that kid had almost been ready to drop out, it teaches me something.

I remember one day in my peer mentor class when one of my favorite administrators, whom I had always viewed as a very nice man, came in angrier than I had ever seen him. He was fuming about what some of the younger girls had done. I followed him out of the room and told him to come to me if he wanted any help with making sure the freshman girls I mentored were on track. He said okay and walked away.

Later that day he told me I was the only reason those girls did not get suspended. Knowing I had helped them was a huge boost for my morale. Even though they may not graduate or may not remember who I am, they will never be able to say they couldn't find anyone to help them.

All the way along, my parents help me by constantly talking and listening. I cannot remember a day when my mom has not forced me to relate a good thing that happened at school, and something I learned. I will always be grateful for that.

My parents have also told every adult who has ever been in charge of me that that person had total permission to discipline me. It is something that has always stuck in my mind—and I know my parents have always had a reason for wanting me to act right.

Your local public school is like life—it does not have the option of choosing who walks through the front door, just as you do not choose who will walk into your life tomorrow. But you do choose how that person will influence the rest of your life.

To parents who have kids in public school, I would say, live out what you believe. Dads, it is important to me to know that every morning my dad prays for a hedge of protection around me, that only God's will be done. I do not even need to hear it in order to believe he is praying that prayer every day. It is something I hold in my heart when I jump in and break up a fight, or when more than half of my friends get suspended. My parents always pray that we kids will use our hallways as a mission field for Christ. I think about that a lot.

Also, parents, encourage your older kids to help your younger ones. In the early years of parenting, your older children will be your "practice kids," but they too learn from your mistakes and can pass on the wisdom. I cannot count how many times I have called one of my three older siblings to ask for their advice. I strive to be that for my four younger siblings.

At the end of the day, when the home is a safe place, that is the biggest factor for feeling safe in the mission field of public school.